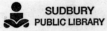

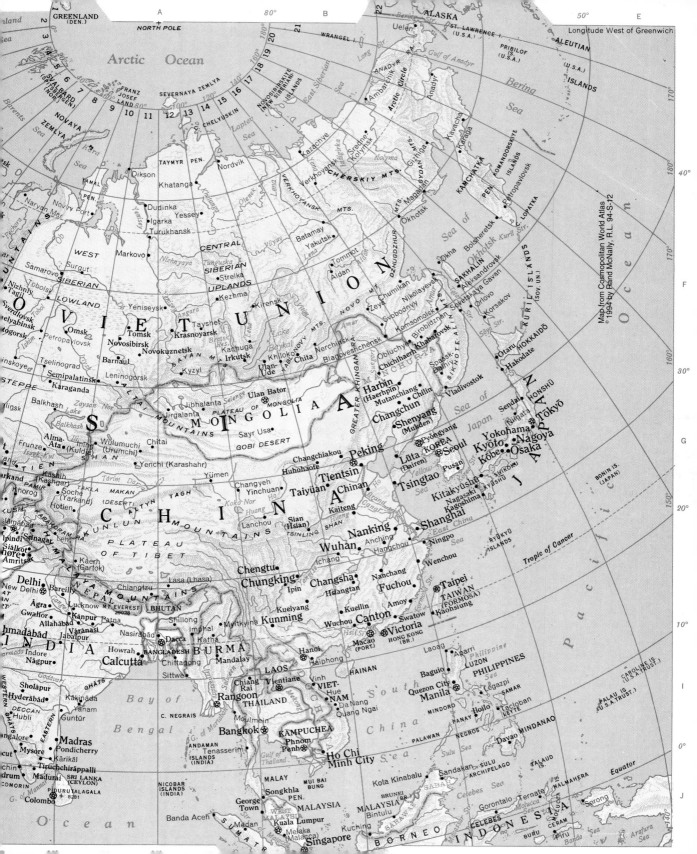

Enchantment of the World

TAIWAN

By Alice Cromie

with a contribution by Parris H. Chang

Consultant for Taiwan: Senator Parris H. Chang, Ph.D., Member of the Legislative Yuan (Parliament), Republic of China, Taiwan; Professor of Political Science, Director, Center for East Asian Studies, Pennsylvania State University, University Park, Pennsylvania

Consultant for Reading: Robert L. Hillerich, Ph.D., Professor Emeritus, Bowling Green State University, Bowling Green, Ohio; Consultant, Pinellas County Schools, Florida

CHILDRENS PRESS®
CHICAGO

Primary schoolchildren enjoy a class outing.

Project Editor: Mary Reidy
Design: Margrit Fiddle

Library of Congress Cataloging-in-Publication Data

Cromie, Alice.
    Taiwan / by Alice Cromie.
        p.   cm. – (Enchantment of the world)
    Includes index.
    Summary: Discusses the geography, history, government,
economics, people, and culture of this island nation.
    ISBN 0-516-02627-5
    1. Taiwan–Juvenile literature.   [1.   Taiwan.]
I. Title. II. Series.
DS799.C76   1994   94-6120
951.24'9–dc20   CIP
                                                      AC

Picture Acknowledgments
AP/Wide World Photos: 27 (right), 28 (left), 60 (bottom
right), 107
ASIA Visuals: © **Cheryl Sheridan,** 14, 56 (bottom left), 79
(bottom left)
The Bettmann Archive: 18, 23, 74

Cameramann International, Ltd.: Cover, 4, 8, 32, 32 (inset),
33, 34 (inset), 36, 36 (inset), 37 (left), 38, 39, 40, 41, 42
(right), 44, 45, 46 (2 photos), 56 (top and bottom right), 60
(top and bottom left), 62, 63, 65, 66 (2 photos), 67, 69, 70,
73 (left), 79 (bottom right), 82, 84, 89, 91, 92, 93, 95 (left),
96, 103, 105 (2 photos), 112 (2 photos)
© **Alice Cromie:** 28 (right), 79 (top)
H. Armstrong Roberts: © **M. Roessler,** 37 (right)
© **Norma Morrison:** 51 (2 photos), 56 (center right)
Photri: 6
© **Porterfield/Chickering:** 5, 13, 15, 20, 42 (left), 43, 48, 53,
58 (2 photos), 73 (right), 86, 89 (right)
Reuters/Bettmann: 29, 95 (right), 109 (2 photos), 113
Root Resources: © **Constance Wilhere,** 10; © **Byron Crader,**
55 (left)
Stock Montage: 21, 24
Tony Stone Images: © **Geoff Tompkinson,** 30, 35, 52, 102
SuperStock International, Inc.: © **Charles Marden Fitch,**
34; © **Steve Vidler,** 55 (right); © **Frank Wen,** 76; © **David
Forbert,** 98
Travel Stock: © **Donna Carroll,** 9, 50
UPI/Bettmann Newsphotos: 25 (2 photos), 27 (left)
Valan: © **Jeff Foott,** 99; © **M. Magivahanan,** 101 (left);
© **Paul Janosi:** 101 (right)
Len W. Meents: Maps on 50, 52, 56, 58
**Courtesy Flag Research Center, Winchester,
Massachusetts 01890:** Flag on back cover
Cover: A street in the center of downtown Taipei

Ami women in their native costume

TABLE OF CONTENTS

A village nestled in a lush valley near Taipei

Chapter 1

BEAUTIFUL ISLE

Legend has it that one day in 1590 a Portuguese galleon in the far Pacific sighted a body of land. The land was graced with white sandy beaches. Coastal plains covered with lush green vegetation swept back from the sea to deep forests. Mountain peaks rose dramatically above the fleecy clouds.

The Portuguese sailors gathered on the ocean-battered decks of their vessel and cried, *"Ihla formosa! Ihla formosa!"* "Beautiful isle! Beautiful isle!" Most of the names mariners gave to the lands they discovered have been lost in the mists of time. However, one officer recorded the discovery when he returned to the Western world. The island was known as Formosa for centuries.

Now it is called *Taiwan*, meaning "Terraced Bay," as it was thousands of years before Europeans saw the land. Since 1949, when the Chinese Nationalists (Kuomintang, or KMT) relocated their government here, Taiwan has been the site of the Republic of China (ROC). Situated at the crossroads of one of the busiest air

Lotus plants in Taipei's Botanical Gardens

routes in the Far East, Taiwan is surrounded by five bodies of water: (clockwise from the north) the East China Sea; the Philippine Sea, part of the Pacific Ocean; the Bashi Channel between Taiwan and Luzon in the Philippines; the South China Sea; and the Formosa (or Taiwan) Strait between mainland China and Taiwan.

The main island of Taiwan is 235 miles (378 kilometers) long and 90 miles (145 kilometers) wide at its widest point. Taiwan, including the Pescadores Islands, has an area of 13,900 square miles (36,000 square kilometers). It is shaped like a tobacco leaf, though a lotus leaf might seem more fitting. The legendary lotus leaf is a Buddhist symbol for an "Enlightened Man." Lotus plants fill the ponds of Taipei's Botanical Gardens and other decorative pools throughout the long summer. Taipei is the political as well as the commercial capital of Taiwan.

New and old
styles of architecture
are found
side by side.

Taiwan is about the size of the Netherlands or, roughly, of Maryland and Delaware together. Its offshore islands include Quemoy, Matsu, Lutao, Lanyu, and the *Pescadores*, meaning "fishermen" in Portuguese. A total of eighty-four offshore islands are under Taiwan's jurisdiction.

The island of Taiwan straddles the Tropic of Cancer and is almost equidistant from Shanghai and Hong Kong (one-and-a-half hours by jet). It lies about the same latitude as Hawaii, so it is not surprising to find pineapple and sugarcane being cultivated.

Today's population is more than twenty million. Temples, forested mountains, and fertile fields can be found here. In the capital city of Taipei, steel-and-glass highrises shine above gracefully styled Chinese buildings such as the ones Marco Polo found in China centuries ago. All of this and more helps Taiwan to live up to its name–the Beautiful Isle.

Dawn in the Yu Shan (Jade Mountain)

Chapter 2

THE MOUNTAINOUS
LAND

Taiwan is part of a chain of islands that lies close to the Asian continent. It marks the edge of the Asiatic Continental Shelf. It is the largest body of land between Japan and the Philippines.

Mountains and foothills cover two-thirds of the island. There are sixty-two peaks rising more than 10,000 feet (3,048 meters). The loftiest of these is Yu Shan (*shan* means "mountain" in Mandarin Chinese), also known as Jade Mountain and Mt. Morrison. It soars to a majestic 13,113 feet (3,997 meters).

CLIMATE

Summer storms often bring heavy rainfall. The tropical cyclones, known in East Asia as typhoons, usually strike in July, August, and September. These can be accompanied by winds up to 150 miles (241 kilometers) an hour, which can cause heavy damage to crops, uproot trees, set off landslides, and capsize cargo ships in the harbor. There is, however, ample warning of these destructive winds, and shelters are available. Experienced residents are quick to prepare for these storms, and city structures usually escape severe damage.

Humidity is high during the long summer, and the brief winters are relatively mild, though cold drizzling rains may occur. In the coldest months snow blankets the highest mountain peaks. Because of the warm and humid climate, most flowers bloom all year. Gentle spring rains sometimes seem to create a mystical effect in the many gardens of Taipei and other cities.

THE RICH SEA PLAINS

Because Taiwan lies off the east coast of Asia and is bisected by the Tropic of Cancer, it has the benefit of warm ocean currents and a climate that is both subtropical, with an average temperature of just under 71 degrees Fahrenheit (22 degrees Celsius) in the north, and tropical, with an average of 76 degrees Fahrenheit (24 degrees Celsius) in the south. This allows the profitable and, in some cases, yearlong cultivation of rice, sugarcane, pineapples, oranges, papayas, watermelons, bananas, and other valued fruits and staples. Fishing, too, is plentiful, with a surplus to supply other markets as well as satisfy domestic needs. There are many picturesque and busy fishing villages, particularly along the northeast coast.

THE CHUNGYANG SHANMO

The *Chungyang Shanmo,* "central range," of mountains was formed when prehistoric volcanoes raised the land out of the sea. Coral formations embedded in rock may still be found at 2,000

A man fishing off the coral reefs of the southern coast

feet (610 meters) above sea level. Off the southern coast lie coral reefs that were built up during the Pleistocene Period, about ten thousand years ago, near the end of the Ice Age.

Volcanoes, which are inactive these days, provide hot mineral waters for a series of spas along the crest of the Chungyang Shanmo. These are not only invigorating and pleasurable, but often have medicinal qualities said to relieve even chronic ailments.

The Chungyang Shanmo runs roughly parallel to the coastline. There is a sharp descent to the Pacific Ocean on the east and terraced tablelands and alluvial coastal plains on the west. Along the western coast the climate is tropical, and tropical vegetation stretches across the plains into the foothills. Beyond the foothills, the growth of timber climbs the mountainside. Yu Shan, just above the Tropic of Cancer, is snow crowned from December to May. It is sometimes called "the hat of Taiwan." The Yu Shan National Park is a wildlife preserve.

The Tamsui River

RIVERS, THE OCEAN, FORESTS, AND WATERFALLS

From the southern tip of the island to the northern headlands there are hundreds of short brisk rivers. No inland point is more than fifty miles (eighty kilometers) from the sea. The steep cliffs on the eastern side of the Chungyang Shanmo make the shore very narrow at times. Here the ocean may be 6,000 feet (1,829 meters) deep. This depth, plus strong ocean currents, prevents alluvial deposits like those that have built up the western coastline.

Although the island once was entirely forested, only about 60 percent of Taiwan is tree covered today. Early settlers found a wealth of exotic and useful woods: rattan, camphor, cedar, oak, pine, and others. Bamboo has been profitable in many ways. Bamboo groves are found in forests and also in farm plantings.

Among the heavily forested mountains are plunging waterfalls below skies that deepen to purple at sunset. Hovering layers of misty clouds seem so serene one may feel as if one has stepped into a Chinese painting.

Opposite page: A waterfall in Taroko Gorge

Chapter 3

IN THE PAST

Though historians often disagree, some archaeologists believe that prehistoric man first appeared on Taiwan more than ten thousand years ago. The earliest aborigines may have come from Malaysia, Polynesia, and the south of China. Tools, fossils, and other artifacts excavated in western Taiwan and the Pescadores are very like those discovered on the Chinese mainland.

THE LAND OF YINGCHOW

Here, as elsewhere, exact dates relating to the distant dawn of time and culture are problematic. The most ancient Chinese reference to the island indicates it was known as the "Land of Yingchow" around 200 B.C. An early record indicates there was an attempt to explore the island, but the first attempt to establish a Chinese claim to the land probably did not take place until early in the third century A.D.

The Kingdom of Wu, from the south of China, sent an expedition of some ten thousand men across the Formosa Strait. When Genghis Khan, the Mongol land-and-power grabber, founded the Yuan Dynasty on the Chinese mainland in 1206, the island of Taiwan came under the control of the Chinese Empire.

In 1430 Cheng Ho, a well-known Chinese magistrate and navigator from the Ming court, returned from his travels and reported that he had visited a beautiful island not far offshore from southern China. It was recorded as Taiwan. The emperor, however, had prohibited emigration from his kingdom. Not until the first quarter of the seventeenth century did large groups of mainland Chinese begin to explore and settle on the island.

RAIDERS, TRADERS, AND INVADERS

The lure of a fruitful and forested land, coupled with rumors of riches to be gained from precious metals and gems, brought pirates and other adventurers to Taiwan. During the fifteenth and sixteenth centuries, despite the Ming prohibition against settlement beyond its boundaries, some Chinese pioneers managed to migrate to the island. They hoped to take advantage of its natural resources in coal, exotic woods, sulfur, iron, jade, opals, and coral.

Both Chinese and Japanese pirates made the island their base and attacked ships on the China seas. Taiwan's location on the major shipping lanes of East Asia was ideal for such raids.

THE DUTCH TAKE OVER

In 1593 Japan tried to occupy Taiwan but failed. Then came the Dutch, who had lost in their efforts to wrest the city of Macao on mainland China from the Portuguese. The Dutch settled on Taiwan's southern coast in 1624 and built three forts. The remains of one of these, Fort Zeelandia, are still standing today.

The Dutch found a large number of Chinese settlers already busily exporting deerskin, meat, sugar, and rice. The newcomers

A photo taken around 1890 shows an aborigine headhunter.

set up trading stations and used Chinese labor to build churches as well as fortifications. The Dutch introduced heavy taxes and labor restrictions. They then imported zealous missionaries to convert the populace to Christianity.

About the same time, Spanish adventurers landed at the city now known as Keelung (or Chilung). They occupied the northern coastal areas until they were driven out by the Dutch in 1641. Meanwhile, the powerful and enterprising Dutch East India Company began to import opium from Java, an island in the Netherlands East Indies, now Indonesia. The Chinese learned how to mix the opium with tobacco and smoke it.

ABORIGINES AND HAKKAS

Some of the aborigines on the island roamed the mountains and hunted black bears, monkeys, wild boar, gibbons, lizards, flying squirrels, and other wild animals. Many of these people were headhunters. Headhunting continued in some areas until the

Japanese, taking colonial control near the end of the nineteenth century, stopped the practice.

Other early groups occupied the rich plains of the southwest and were fairly settled tillers of the soil. Some, however, used the slash-and-burn method of agriculture (similar to modern strip mining), which soon wore out the soil and forced the people to move on. Other aborigines were fishermen along the coast.

The earliest Chinese to settle on the island were the Hakkas, a persecuted minority group. The Hakkas had been driven from their homes in northern Honan Province in China. *Hakka* means "guest" or "stranger." As they tried to gain a foothold on the productive coastal plains, the Hakkas pushed the aborigines inland toward the mountains.

Later, further migrations from the mainland were spurred by the revolt against the Manchus from Manchuria, who had conquered the Ming Dynasty. The Mings had lasted nearly three centuries but had fallen into corruption and political weakness toward the last quarter of the seventeenth century. Just as the Hakkas had pushed the aborigines back from the coast, so the newly arrived Chinese pushed the Hakkas toward the mountains and away from the richest land and fishing waters.

The majority of ethnic Chinese in Taiwan today descend from these seventeenth-century settlers, who gave themselves the name *ben-di-ren*, "this-place-person," to distinguish themselves from the Hakkas and the aborigines. Later this name helped separate them from the political refugees of 1949, whom they called *wai-sheng-ren*, "outer-province-people." Like many native American Indians and the aborigines of Australia, most of Taiwan's aborigines now live in government-designated areas. The Taiwanese aborigines live in the mountains of central and southern Taiwan.

An Atayal woman wearing a colorful outfit and the customary layers of necklaces, as well as a headdress

Nine of the nineteen original groups maintain their ethnic identities and continue their ancient customs (except headhunting). These are the Ami, Atayal, Paiwan, Pingpu, Yami, Lukai, Peinan, Saihsia, and Taiyu. Slash-and-burn farming is still practiced by some. Others still hunt in the mountains, while some cultivate alpine fruit orchards to supply Taiwan's markets, which have a lucrative trade in gourmet foods. Aborigine women dress in brightly woven fabrics and wear multiple layers of necklaces. Some women may wear headdresses. Many males wear Western-style jeans and T-shirts.

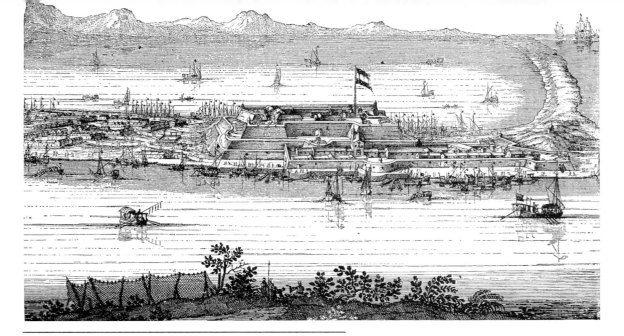

A sixteenth-century drawing of a Dutch fortress in Taiwan

AN EARLY HERO

The Ming Dynasty of mainland China lasted for almost three hundred years under sixteen emperors from 1356 to 1644. As the arts and sciences of the Ming began to fade under corruption at court, the Manchus tried to seize control. Before hanging himself, the last Ming emperor named a Taiwan-based pirate, Cheng Chi-lung, to command what remained of the Ming forces. Cheng had a Japanese wife who bore him a son. This young man, Cheng Cheng-kung, became known to the West as Koxinga. He developed an army of more than ten thousand men and a fleet of some three thousand war junks (Chinese ships) and fought the Manchus for more than a decade. He came close to recapturing the southern Chinese capital of Nanking, but was forced back by the overwhelming force of the Manchus. Koxinga and his forces retreated to Taiwan in 1658.

In 1661, with reinforcements and a larger fleet, Koxinga began a siege against the Dutch, who had occupied Taiwan for thirty-seven years. The siege continued for nearly two years until Koxinga was victorious. He allowed the Dutch governor and his surviving men to leave the island with their possessions.

Koxinga died only a year after his conquest, at the age of thirty-eight, but he is a national hero and today is venerated in Taiwan as a *chun tzu*, "perfect man." He is considered the founding father of Chinese civilization on the island. As Chiang Kai-shek, the president of the Republic of China, would do many years later, Koxinga brought scholars, teachers, artists, poets, and monks to Taiwan to establish Chinese culture on the island.

Koxinga's son and grandson continued to rule Taiwan until 1684, when the Manchus from mainland China invaded and conquered Taiwan. Taiwan officially became a prefecture of Fukien Province in China, which gave the island its first formal status as an integral part of China. The rule from distant Beijing, the capital of China, was nominal at best, and most islanders continued to do as they pleased. Although there were restrictions against further emigration to Taiwan, more and more mainlanders managed to cross the strait. Despite the Manchu decree, Taiwan's population increased sevenfold.

WEALTH AND WAYWARDNESS

A Prussian missionary, Karl Gutzlaff, who visited Taiwan in 1831, observed: "The island has flourished greatly since it has been in the possession of the Chinese. The rapidity with which this island has been colonized, and the advantage it affords for the colonists to throw off their allegiance, have induced the Chinese to adopt strict measures. The colonists are wealthy and unruly."

*In 1895, at the end of the first Sino-Japanese War,
Japanese troops began a fifty-year occupation.*

For nearly a century while the Manchus held sway, Taiwan stayed aloof from the outside world. Western imperialism eventually ended the isolation. By a treaty between the British and Chinese, four island ports were opened to foreign trade. Westerners lost no time in taking advantage of the new markets at Keelung and Suao in the north and T'ainan and Kaohsiung in the south.

Shipwrecked sailors who were "lucky" enough to be washed ashore soon found they had not reached an island "paradise." They were beaten, imprisoned, and often beheaded either by Chinese authorities or by the aborigines. Beijing refused to take any action against these atrocities, and Western powers resorted to "gunboat diplomacy," dealing directly with the islanders instead of Beijing.

In 1886 Taiwan at last became a province of China. The population then was about 2.5 million. At the conclusion of the first Sino-Japanese (Chinese-Japanese) War in 1895, the island was

British Prime Minister Winston Churchill and United States President Franklin D. Roosevelt met during World War II to discuss the war in the Pacific.

ceded to Japan. During the next fifty years of Japanese occupation some improvements were made, but there also were more than one hundred uprisings against the rulers.

The Japanese advocated literacy and established a comprehensive educational system. Japanese rule also increased agricultural production and created a modern transportation network and the beginnings of an industrial state. When the Japanese were defeated and surrendered at the end of World War II, they had to return the Pescadores to Manchuria and Taiwan to China. During the war Chiang Kai-shek, the leader of the Chinese Nationalists; Franklin D. Roosevelt, president of the United States; and Winston Churchill, prime minister of England, had agreed on

*Mao Zedong (left) opposed the election of
Chiang Kai-shek (right) as president.*

the return of these territories when Japan was defeated. On
October 25, 1945, Taiwan was restored to China.

After World War II, fighting continued in mainland China—this
time in a civil war between the Communists and the Nationalists.
In March 1948 Chiang was elected president of China by the
National Assembly, but the Communists led by Mao Zedong
began winning major military victories. On December 7, 1949,
Chiang and more than two million refugees fled across Formosa
Strait to the island of Taiwan and established the "provisional"
government of the Republic of China (ROC).

Mao won the civil war and established the People's Republic of
China, a Communist regime, on the mainland.

Chapter 4

AN INDEPENDENT
ISLAND NATION

Chiang had learned much from past mistakes on the mainland. With the assistance of American advisers, sweeping land reforms were carried out in Taiwan. Instead of killing dispossessed landlords, the Nationalists paid for their lost acreages and allowed them to invest in Taiwan's economic future.

More reforms were implemented. The education system was modernized. Thousands of students went to the United States to learn new technology and scientific methods that were proving successful in the West.

The United States-Republic of China mutual defense treaty of 1954 provided for Taiwan's security against Communist China's military threat. With United States technical assistance, economic aid, and the American markets, which imported as much as one-third of Taiwan's exports, Taiwan's economy grew rapidly.

Chiang never accepted his defeat at the hands of the Communists in the civil war. Throughout his life he was

Chiang (left) died in 1975 and was succeeded as president by Yen Chia-Kan (above).

determined to recapture the Chinese mainland through military conquest. Thus, in the name of emergency due to the civil war, Chiang maintained a highly repressive rule in Taiwan, with limited representative institutions at local levels.

The Chinese Communists believed they were the rightful government and Taiwan was one of their provinces. The Chinese Nationalists believed that the KMT, the Kuomintang, was the legitimate government of Taiwan and mainland China. In 1971 the UN expelled the Nationalist government of China, which had been a charter member of the world body since 1945. Instead, China's seat went to the Communist government, the People's Republic of China.

Whereas Taiwan's economic development took off during Chiang's reign, Taiwan remained very much a garrison state in which martial law was in effect, the political opposition was suppressed, and people's constitutional rights and political freedoms were severely restricted.

In April 1975 President Chiang died during his fifth term in office. Yen Chia-kan, vice-president since 1966, took the oath of

Left: Chiang Ching-kuo, Chiang Kai-shek's eldest son, served as president from 1978 until his death in 1988.   Right: Dr. Lee Teng-hui, who became president in 1988, is the first native-born president.

office as the president. But the real power went to Chiang Kai-shek's eldest son, Chiang Ching-kuo, then serving as premier. He took his father's place as the chairman of the KMT. In March 1978 he was elected president of the ROC by the National Assembly and Yen stepped down.

Chiang Ching-kuo had held a number of important offices, and as premier in 1972 he led the government in major construction projects. Having taken giant strides toward economic prosperity in his first term as president, he instituted major political reforms in his second term. He lifted martial law, in effect since 1949; removed the ban on new political parties, thereby opening the door for a multiparty political system; lifted restrictions on daily newspapers; and began to rejuvenate the structure of the national parliament to admit younger members. President Chiang Ching-kuo died on January 13, 1988, after a long bout with diabetes.

Vice-President Lee Teng-hui, age sixty-five, was sworn in as the nation's president a few hours later on the same day. Dr. Lee was the first native-born president of the island nation.

A highway under construction in 1992 was part of Taiwan's expansion.

PUTTING AN EDUCATION TO WORK

Early in his career at the Joint Commission on Rural Reconstruction, Lee helped with health programs, modern irrigation, mechanization, and farmers' cooperatives to aid Taiwan's transition from an agricultural to a manufacturing economy. Later as Taipei's mayor he computerized the city government and made extensive use of the citizen advisory panels to monitor development.

Lee also launched a reservoir project that alleviated Taipei's chronic water shortage. Today there are many multipurpose dams and reservoirs that have been developed to provide power as well as irrigation. Some power also is available from three nuclear plants.

Miles of new freeways and the setting up of new sewage disposal plants helped to protect the fast-growing capital city during the rapid expansion of industry. Lee continued such projects during his four years as governor of Taiwan province.

Taipei's streets are a jungle of traffic, people, and signs.

Chapter 5

A JUNGLE ON WHEELS

Some visitors to Taiwan expect to find a tropical Garden of Eden as it looked to the Portuguese sailors of long ago. Others, who have seen countless labels reading "Made in Taiwan" on their own clothing or household furnishings, may look for factories with operators busily running sewing machines; tailors taping measurements for quickly made silk suits; and rows of smocked workers at spinning pottery wheels making vases and lamps. All of these can be found at various sites, but probably the first impression a jet-lagged newcomer will have is of noise, bustling crowds, and traffic.

Most travelers arrive at Chiang Kai-shek International Airport in Taoyuan in northern Taiwan about twenty-five miles (forty kilometers) from Taipei. Not long after it was built, there was a need for expansion. A second terminal with airfreight facilities and a new passenger and air cargo terminal at Hsiao-kang International Airport in Kaohsiung in southern Taiwan will be under construction soon.

At a major intersection in Kaohsiung, a pedestrian bridge makes it possible for people to cross the street safely. Inset: It is common to see automobiles parked illegally on the sidewalks in Taipei.

Taxis take visitors to their destination. The driver will be extremely courteous to his passenger, but he may occasionally erupt with a torrent of Chinese words at other drivers who are trying to use his space. In Chinese the rule at the wheel is *heng-hsian kung-hou* which means "Fight to be first, fear to be last."

This applies in the city also. An editorial in the *Free China Review* takes an entertaining view of it: "When Taipei drivers get behind the wheel they become superbly creative in circumventing traffic laws in order to keep moving. . . . Double-parked cars are everywhere, even in front of police stations. . . . Of course, there are still rules: Look both ways before jumping a red light. Never make an illegal turn if you have to run over a traffic policeman to complete it."

The government has many plans to solve what is considered a number-one problem. Not long ago the Taipei police chief said: "It's a jungle out there." Sorting out the daily traffic of a city of

The New Taipei Park, south of the main railroad station in Taipei, is a popular place to relax.

more than 3.5 million commuters, well over one-half million cars, 3,200 buses, 700,000 motor scooters, and 40,000 taxis admittedly is a chore. "There are less than seven hundred traffic police in Taipei and five hundred are out in the streets every day. Half of them handle traffic accidents, which occur about every five minutes on the average. The other half conduct traffic during rush hours, issue about 7,000 to 8,000 tickets a day, and tow away 1,500 illegally parked cars daily."

In Taipei buses are gaily decorated and there are many colorful costumes to be seen on the streets. It looks as if a parade has gotten tangled in traffic. For pedestrians there are plenty of underpasses for crossing the busiest streets.

Despite the congestion in downtown Taipei, wide tree-lined boulevards grace the government district and the less commercial areas. Also there are enticing public gardens with flower-edged paths, charming Chinese-style little bridges across lotus-filled ponds, graceful pavilions, and teahouses.

The Keelung River flows through Taipei (above). Many buildings, like Taipei City Hall (right), are ultra modern.

A BURGEONING METROPOLIS

Geologists say the site of Taipei was a vast lake in ancient times, but the lake dried up after thousands of years. The Tamsui, Hsintien, and Keelung (or Chilung) rivers flow through the basin where the lake once was.

An American scholar, Daniel Reid, came to live in Taiwan in 1973 when one lone skyscraper rose over the weathered and much-used buildings that housed most of the populace. He remembers vividly:

"The airport was still in town, and the streets had only recently been paved. The ceaseless clatter of pedicabs, pushcarts, and ox-drawn wagons" had just begun to give way to today's vehicles. Now, as Dr. Reid observes:

Taipei's skyline is a sparkling forest of glass-and-steel towers that reflect the latest modern architecture. Big blimps float fatly over the city, advertising the new office buildings and

A shop that sells items used in folk medicine

condominiums to which they are anchored. Cadillacs and
Mercedes-Benz ply the new tree-lined boulevards of East
Taipei, delivering well-heeled occupants to stylish European
boutiques and the splendid lobbies of palatial new hotels. . . .
To accommodate Taipei's teeming traffic, highways and
flyways, over-passes and by-passes gird the burgeoning
metropolis with an ever more complex maze of asphalt.

In the oldest section of town, where some buildings date from
the late nineteenth century, tiny old ladies squat protectively by
baskets of dried food for sale: squid, shrimp, seaweeds,
mushrooms, and other goods.

Other street stands and shops carry spices, cashews, bamboo
utensils, oil paper lanterns, and handwoven baskets. In Snake
Alley one may be startled to see a living curtain of snakes and to
learn that the reptiles are for sale—for food or medical use, not for

Speeding traffic passes the Shihlin Night Market area, which is popular among students because of its bargain prices. Inset: In this restaurant in Snake Alley, diners select the food they want before it is cooked.

pets. The city's largest night market in Hua Hsi Street in the Wanhua district has salespeople, who like old-time carnival barkers, invite shoppers to step right up and try some fresh cobra gall and blood to discover an instant improvement in their eyesight.

Many markets come alive only when the sun sets. And Taipei at night, with its dazzling neon characters, is like a giant carnival. Dozens and dozens of food stalls offer gastronomic specialties prepared for ready consumption; other vendors may have clothing, kitchenware, toys, jewelry, and a bit of everything, including electronic calculators. Rich and poor alike sit on long wooden benches enjoying from the same pots such choice items as

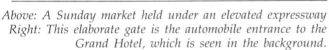

Above: A Sunday market held under an elevated expressway
Right: This elaborate gate is the automobile entrance to the
Grand Hotel, which is seen in the background.

shark's fin stew, dumplings, oyster-rice noodles, and other delicacies. There are fortune-tellers, portrait painters, masseurs, and others ready to serve the buyer.

THE MYRIAD SITES AND SCENES OF A SOPHISTICATED CITY

One of the many impressive buildings is the majestic Grand Hotel on Round Hill with what is said to be the world's largest classical Chinese roof. Madame Chiang Kai-shek supervised its construction, and it is a truly unforgettable experience to stroll through the vast lobby with its high ceilings, red and gold decor, and the mystical ambiance of a Chinese imperial palace.

Taipei is one of the most intriguing cities in the world and is said to be the fastest growing city in Asia.

The National Palace Museum is in a northern suburb of Taipei.

THE NATIONAL PALACE MUSEUM

Taipei has many outstanding museums and temples filled with ancient treasures brought from the mainland. The National Palace Museum is one of the world's great treasuries of art objects. The beginnings of this vast collection may be traced back to the early Sung Dynasty—more than a thousand years. Called "The Treasure House of the Centuries," it is an imposing complex of buff-colored brick buildings with green and yellow slate roofs. It is located in the suburb of Wai-shuang-hsi in the foothills behind the Grand Hotel. The building is actually built into a hillside.

With its landscaped setting, graceful walls, and sweeping stairs, it looks like a palace. Millions of visitors have enjoyed its displays since it was opened to the public in 1965. It has more than

Two women admire ancient Chinese art in the National Palace Museum.

one-quarter million art pieces to be exhibited. If these were changed every three months it would take ten years to show the whole collection. What is not on display is stored in vaults built into the mountain. There are more than 4,000 bronzes, 3,000 jade items, 25,000 porcelain objects, 6,000 paintings and examples of calligraphy, and some 150,000 rare books. Amazingly, this collection is only one-fifth of the treasures originally in China's Forbidden City. The works of art were removed to escape the invading Japanese and destruction from civil war. For sixteen years some thirty scholars and workers carried nearly 20,000 huge cases of these priceless art objects across China in circuitous routes until they could be shipped to Taiwan. It is said that not one piece was broken.

The National Museum of History

MUSEUMS, TEMPLES, AND SHRINES

The National Museum of History has more than ten thousand art objects that date from 2000 B.C. to the present. It houses artifacts that were returned to China by Japan at the end of World War II and many artifacts unearthed in mainland China. Plans are to present a comprehensive view of life in old Cathay (China), including items related to dress, food, housing, ceremonies, religion, and entertainment. The museum shows works of foreign and contemporary Chinese artists. Located in downtown Taipei, it is administered by the ministry of education.

The exterior and grounds of the Taipei Fine Arts Museum

The Taipei Fine Arts Museum is the largest of its kind in Asia. Its exhibition halls surround a central courtyard like stacked cubes, permitting maximum sunlight. The three-story lobby accommodates large sculptures, and the galleries are filled with paintings by renowned international as well as local artists.

There are many other fine museums in the city that cover a variety of interests. Among these are the National Revolutionary Martyrs Shrine, the Taiwan Provincial Museum, the Postal Museum, the Chung-cheng Aviation Museum, and New Taipei Park—which is busy even at dawn as hundreds of vendors spread their wares on blankets on the grassy grounds. Two nineteenth-century locomotives on view are part of the first railway.

Inside the Chiang Kai-shek Memorial Hall (left)
is a bronze statue of President Chiang Kai-shek (right).

CHIANG KAI-SHEK MEMORIAL HALL

The stately, beautiful building, massive but graceful, that commemorates the late president Chiang Kai-shek is set in formal gardens. The memorial is white, the Chinese color of mourning. The Cultural Center also contains the National Theater and the National Concert Hall. The vast main hall rises to a height of 250 feet (76 meters). On the ground floor exhibition rooms with memorabilia include a theater that shows documentary films of the late president. On the second floor an imposing 25-ton (22,680-kilogram) statue of Chiang Kai-shek is on display.

Lungshan Temple is dedicated to Kuan Yin, the Buddhist goddess of mercy.

"DRAGON MOUNTAIN"

Lungshan Temple is the oldest, most famous of Taiwan's many temples and possibly the busiest. It is often called "Dragon Mountain" because a great many of the sculptured creatures, looking ferocious, line the fluted roof and the large pillars indoors. Located in a now congested section of old Taipei, it was built in the eighteenth century to honor Kuan Yin, the goddess of mercy, and Matsu, the goddess of the sea. The interior is scented with burning incense, the aroma of many candles lit in supplication of the gods, paper "money" burning in huge pots, and food offerings to the gods. Soft chatter among the suppliants and the shuffle of many feet never cease.

*The Chinese celebrate Confucius' birthday, also called
Teachers' Day, at the Confucius Temple. Teachers are in purple
and students in yellow.*

A TEMPLE TO A WISE MAN

The Temple of Confucius in Taipei is in a classical compound
on the northern outskirts of the city. It has a beautifully designed
Chinese roof of glazed yellow tile and a lovely and tranquil
interior befitting the virtues of peace and quiet taught by the wise
man centuries ago. The courtyards and grottos are connected by
moon-shaped gates and garden paths.

Military units stand for review in front of the Presidential Building on National Day.

THE NERVE CENTER OF IT ALL

The administrative center of the government is the Presidential Building in the heart of the city. The plaza fronting the building holds enormous crowds during celebrations. On National Day (October 10), which is the "Double Tenth" festival, the Presidential Building and the Grand Hotel are ablaze with dazzling lights and decorations.

Above: A road winds along the rugged coast of northern Taiwan.
Below: The Sun Yat-sen Freeway ends at the port of Keelung.

Chapter 6

A BEAUTIFUL ISLAND

NORTH TAIWAN

North Taiwan is flanked from west to east by the Formosa Strait, the East China Sea, and the Pacific Ocean. Keelung, the second largest of five international seaports, overlooks the East China Sea. It also is the northern terminal of the Sun Yat-sen Freeway and the electrified trunk railroad, both of which extend to Kaohsiung in the southwest part of the island.

Once known as Santissima Trinidad, this northern city has had an eventful history. Trinidad obviously is not a Dutch or Chinese name, so it indicates that the Spanish once were here, at least briefly. In 1626 an expeditionary force arrived from the Philippines. It was driven out in 1642 by the Dutch, who then managed to keep their hold on the land until conquered by the Ming Dynasty loyalist Koxinga.

An earthquake destroyed much of the town in 1867. In August 1884, during a brief war between France and the Chinese, the French bombarded the port and took over Keelung for eight months until peace was restored. In May 1895 the Japanese arrived for a short time. The end came with the death of the

Visitors of all ages enjoy "Window on China." Here they look at a replica of the Forbidden City, built in the fifteenth century, in Beijing, China.

Japanese expeditionary leader, an imperial prince, who succumbed to malaria before his fiftieth birthday.

A huge statue of Kuan Yin, goddess of mercy, overlooks the harbor from a hilltop. Kuan Yin's mercy does not extend to weather: Keelung is one of the wettest cities in the world. The area averages 214 days of rainfall, most of which falls from October to March.

"Window on China," in Taoyuan County not far from Taipei, is a permanent exhibition of miniature models of historical and other notable sites throughout Taiwan and mainland China. The tiny railroads run, the boats move, and the famous Wall of China extends snakelike over hill and dale. It is one of the most impressive and instructive exhibits of its kind in the world for its bird's-eye view of China's major architectural accomplishments.

TAMSUI, YEHLIU, AND WULAI

Situated on the northwest coast, at the confluence of the Tamsui River and the Formosa Strait, Tamsui is a historical city. In the seventeenth century the Spanish built Fort San Domingo on a hilltop. The locals, however, called it *Hung Mao Cheng*, "Fort of the Red-Haired Barbarians." Tamsui and other Spanish holdings in the island were taken by the Dutch and, eventually, restored to China when the Dutch were driven out in 1661. In 1860 the port was opened by the Ch'ing Dynasty to foreign trade. Soon a British consulate was established, but wars and other troubles kept Tamsui a charming fishing village rather than a major port city.

An intriguing legend says that a woman who lived in a fishing village on an island off the coast of Fukien Province about A.D. 690 offered herself in place of a young girl about to be sacrificed to two monsters, a yearly custom. The woman's piety was strong enough to defeat the evil creatures, and she made them her servants when she became Matsu, goddess of the sea. The statues of Matsu's two servants, *Chien Li Yen*, "Thousand Mile Eye," and *Shun Feng Er*, "With the Wind Ear," stand by the altar of the beautiful old Lung Shan Temple. Matsu and her reformed monsters guard sailors and calm the seas. The fishermen of Tamsui usually ask their protection before setting out for the day's catch.

Ching Shui Temple is a short distance from Lung Shan, up a narrow alley through the town market. Again according to legend, Ching Shui was a devout Buddhist who battled with a demon and was badly burned. He is always depicted with a black face. Supposedly a temple robber once broke the nose of Ching Shui's

Tamsui
Taipei
Keelung
Wulai

Unusual rock formations along the shore at Yehliu

statue, and the monks repaired it. Since then, it is said that whenever disaster threatens, Ching Shui's nose drops off.

Tamsui is noted for its fine schools, handicraft shops, antique stores, and splendid sunsets. Above all it is known to the sports-minded for its golf and country club, the oldest in Taiwan and one of the most challenging courses in East Asia, where major tournaments are often held.

Yehliu on the North Coast Highway is a promontory with fantastic rock formations carved by wind and water through the ages. One striking formation is called the Queen's Head because it reminds many visitors of the statues of Nefertiti, a queen of Egypt. The coral shapes may seem like dinosaurs, griffins, various fish, and even Cinderella's famous lost shoe.

A traditional home (left) and costumed aboriginal dancers (right) in Wulai

Wulai, a mountain resort south of Taipei, is the site of a village inhabited by the Atayal aborigines, the second-largest native group in Taiwan. There are handicraft displays and costumed entertainment by the Atayal. A cable-car ride above a deep wooded ravine toward a lovely waterfall on the mountainside is a breath-taking experience.

EAST TAIWAN

The East-West Cross-Island Highway, which took 100,000 workers forty-six months to complete in 1960 and cost nearly $11 million, opened the great Chungyang Shanmo to farming, logging, cattle breeding, and tourism. It has been called "The Rainbow of Treasure Island" and "Asia's Most Beautiful Highway."

Taipei ★
Tungshih ●
Hualien ●
Chungyang Shanmo

Many people travel by bus on the East-West Cross-Island Highway so they can enjoy the spectacular scenery.

The highway runs from the coast of the Pacific Ocean on the east to Tungshih, a gateway opening onto the verdant plains of the west coast, a distance of 120 miles (193 kilometers). In its easternmost section, the highway snakes through Taroko Gorge, a marble-walled canyon that has spectacular overhangs and precipitous plunges. The gorge itself is a 12-mile (19-kilometer) stretch with thirty-eight tunnels, some of which have windows gouged out of solid rock to provide light and ventilation.

Aborigine girls in native Ami costume gather at the eastern entrance to the gorge, considered one of the "Seven Wonders of Asia." At nearby Hualien, performances are given by the Ami. Taroko has recently been made a national park to preserve its natural beauty.

Opposite Page: Taroko Gorge is a magnificent sight.

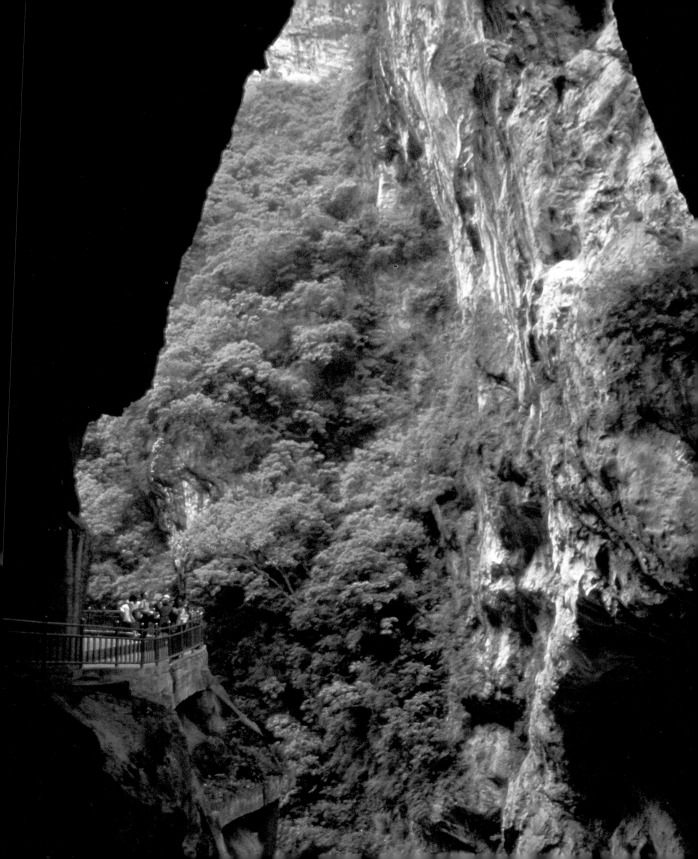

CENTRAL TAIWAN

In 1721 a boatload of emigrants from mainland China settled on the west coast of the island and named their village Tatun, "Big Mound." When the Japanese took over in 1895, they changed the name to *Taichung*, which means "Central Taiwan." Taichung is now an international seaport and the third-largest city in Taiwan.

The original site of the settlement is now Chung-shan (Sun Yat-sen) Park. Taichung is especially proud of its Martyrs Shrine, which was erected in 1970. It is an example of classical Chinese architecture that many consider even more outstanding than similar martyrs' shrines in Taipei or Hualien. It commemorates the sacrifice of seventy-two Chinese patriots who were beheaded in 1911 by the Manchus just before the republican revolution.

Close by the Martyrs Shrine is the Confucian Shrine, which has a very simple design. The shrine is serene except on Confucius's birthday. Then there are colorful ceremonies with ancient costumes and two-thousand-year-old music played on antique instruments.

Almost half the Taiwanese practice the religion of Buddhism. Buddha, who lived in the sixth century, is represented by many images. The fattest Buddha image in Taiwan is in Pao-Chueh Temple on the north side of the city of Taichung. *Milofo*, "The Happy Buddha," is 101 feet (31 meters) high. A small folk craft museum is inside the hollow pedestal of the giant Buddha. There are many other merry Buddhas in the courtyards.

The city of Changhua, southwest of Taichung, is famous for its huge concrete Buddha image on a lotus-shaped platform. Its construction took 300 tons (272,000 kilograms) of concrete.

Sun Moon Lake is a prime resort for honeymooners, but it also attracts thousands of other vacationers. Set in the central

Left: Changhua boasts the world's largest Buddha.
Above: Wen-Wu Temple on Sun Moon Lake

highlands at 2,415 feet (736 meters) above sea level, with its serene blue waters against a frame of tapering mountains, it has often lured poets to describe it. The nine-story *Tzu En*, "Filial Devotion," Pagoda, situated across the lake from the *Wen-Wu*, "Literature Warrior," Temple dedicated to Confucius, stands on the highest elevation of any pagoda in Taiwan.

The two stone lions that guard the Wen-Wu Temple are the largest in the world, but their presence at this "honeymoon lake" is not wholly romantic. They were built at the expense of a wealthy industrialist whose given name, *Ho-shih*, means "lion." This may be compensated for by the statue on Kwanghwa Islet in the lake, where love-beguiled couples who row to the little island at sunset are greeted by a figure wearing brightly colored robes and a magnificent long white beard. He is China's traditional matchmaker, "The Old Man Under the Moon." He has a benevolent smile, but in many Chinese love stories of yesteryear,

Kaohsiung is both an
international seaport
and an industrial center.
Some views of the city
(clockwise from above) are:
loading containers
onto a freighter,
a decorated government
building, baskets of chickens
in an outdoor market,
and a fishing boat
returning from the sea.

the bride's mother, with a determined set to her chin, is the matchmaker.

The Alishan Forest Recreation Area centers on the town of Alishan. It is linked to Chiayi in central Taiwan by a narrow-gauge railway that crosses seventy-seven bridges and goes through fifty tunnels before it reaches Chiayi in Central Taiwan. The station at Alishan is situated at an elevation of 7,185 feet (2,190 meters) and is the highest railroad station in East Asia. Alishan is a favorite resort, with many activities. There is an observation deck on nearby Mt. *Chu*, "Celebration Mountain," to view the Sea of Clouds that rings Yu Shan, which is best seen at sunrise.

Yu Shan posed a slight problem to the Japanese when they took over Taiwan in 1895 because the mountain is loftier than Mt. Fuji, the pride of the Japanese Empire. While the Japanese remained in charge, they changed the name to *Niitakayama*, "New High Mountain."

SOUTH TAIWAN

Kaohsiung is located on the southwest coast, fronting the Formosa Strait. It is the largest international seaport in the Republic of China and is also the chief industrial center. It is one of the world's largest container-handling ports and the site of Taiwan's second international airport. Kaohsiung has developed an export processing zone that often is studied by other countries as a model. Like Taipei, the city has the status of a province, and the mayor is regarded as a provincial governor.

T'ainan, the oldest city in Taiwan, served as capital of the island for more than two hundred years (1684-1887). It was here

*A pool and garden on the grounds of the shrine to Koxinga (left)
and the Confucian Temple (right) in T'ainan*

that Koxinga with his eight thousand troops and three thousand
war junks put an end to the Dutch colonial occupation. The
shrine to Koxinga was built in 1875. Surprisingly, this enterprise
was approved by the emperor on the mainland, who was second
to last of the twelve monarchs of the Ch'ing Dynasty. He had
forgiven his former enemy and recognized him as a national hero.

T'ainan is known as the city of a hundred temples, but the
actual count is 209. The Confucian Temple is the oldest temple in
Taiwan dedicated to Confucius and is architecturally superior to
all others built in his honor. It was built in 1665 by Koxinga's son.
One of the many intriguing details regarding the structure is a
stone tablet on the wall beside the impressive gateway. It reads:

"Officers, civil and military, soldiers and civilians, dismount here." Everyone did just that, then remounted once they were past the entrance. Ancient books, musical instruments, and ceremonial costumes are on display.

One modest-sized temple is of particular interest because it is "The Temple to the Five Concubines," where the remains of the secondary wives of a Ming Dynasty prince are enshrined. In 1683 as the Manchus were planning to invade Taiwan, the prince told his concubines he would commit suicide by hanging rather than live under Manchu rule. The five women donned their best clothes and hanged themselves to be with the prince in the next world. Two days later the prince wrote some poems, concluded his business affairs, and then put on his court robes and invited friends for a farewell dinner. When they departed he took his own life.

Kenting, "Plowmen," National Park originated with the farmers from the mainland who settled in the southernmost part of the island in what is now known as the *Hengchun*, "Eternal Spring," Peninsula. It is flanked by four seas–the Formosa Strait, the South China Sea, the Bashi Channel, and the Pacific Ocean.

Kenting was Taiwan's first national park (1982) intended to preserve and protect the marine and land wonders of the area. Among its wonders are *Maopitou*, "Cat's Nose," an elevation of the coastline that offers a splendid view of the sea. Other natural fascinations of the area are the Stalagmite Cave, Fairy Cave, Silver Dragon Cave, Umbrella Booth, and Reclining Ape Ridge. Kenting's extensive population of tropical flora draws visitors from around the world.

Above: A group of young women, some on motor scooters, meet with their friends.   Below: A lawyer (left) speaks to members of Taoyuan County Rotary Club about difficult court cases and a police officer (right) gives a driver a ticket.

Chapter 7

EVERYDAY LIFE

TAIWAN WOMEN TODAY

Near the end of the twentieth century a feminist movement began growing, and women in Taiwan today are asking far more for themselves than their grandmothers or mothers ever asked. They hold many jobs, as office workers, teachers, editors, policewomen, salespersons, and even cabinet members. In the cities, housewives and working women exercise for fitness in public groups in the park or on sidewalks before their day begins. In recent years there have been many more groups for women to join that help them to have wider scopes of interest.

The tradition that men are breadwinners and women are solely homemakers and child rearers is still entrenched in many families, but Taiwanese women are getting a higher education with the encouragement of the government, competing with men in the work force, and still struggling for equal pay. More and more women, reared to think that wives should be only sweet-tempered, submissive, and devoted to maintaining a smoothly run home and raising obedient children, no longer feel inferior to men. Career women are achieving higher visibility. For example, television in Taiwan has more women then men newscasters.

Primary schoolchildren in uniforms

EDUCATION

Taiwan has one of the highest literacy rates in the world. Education has always been highly valued by the Taiwanese. The government provides free textbooks in the elementary grades and gives grants in rural communities to help establish schools. While many preschools are privately owned and operated, tuition is free in most state-owned kindergartens. These days about 200,000 preschoolers attend more than 1,300 kindergartens, which have about 7,500 teachers.

At present, nine years attendance is compulsory. This may be raised to twelve years. Preschool is optional. The elementary grades are one to six, and junior high is grades seven through nine. The primary subjects are the Chinese language, science, math, civics, art, music, and physical education. As in many other countries, homework is important, and parents must check the

A father helps his son complete a homework assignment.

work daily and sign their children's assignments before the papers can be handed in.

Junior high students must pass a competitive examination to enter high school, and high school seniors must pass an exam before entering college. The junior high years are chiefly spent preparing for the exam. There is special education for the handicapped, disabled, or gifted, and adult education courses in the evenings. Educational television programs are broadcast for students in the higher grades and college.

Nearly 100 percent of elementary school students complete their six years. About 80 percent of junior high students graduate and enter high school after passing the entrance requirements. There are more than a thousand junior and senior high schools in Taiwan with an average attendance of nearly 2 million. More than 500,000 are enrolled in the 121 colleges and universities on the island. There is less than 8 percent illiteracy in Taiwan, and most of the illiterates are more than seventy years old.

THE UNIQUE ART OF CHINESE FOOD:
THE CHINESE DON'T CHOOSE CHOP SUEY

A Taiwan government official and former fighter pilot said, "It [cookery] is an art which has over the centuries ascended from peak to peak and is now at its apex in Taiwan." Most connoisseurs agree that Taipei ranks as the world's greatest Chinese culinary capital. It offers the most variety as well as abundance and quality of Chinese food.

An interesting story is told in Taiwan that Americans of the midnineteenth century invented chop suey. (A scholar and historian in Taipei jestingly declared that few self-respecting Chinese would order the dish, let alone eat it.) During the gold rush days in the American West, miners would visit the camps of the Chinese who served as cheap labor in the region. The miners felt themselves too good to eat at the same table with the Chinese laborers and waited to be served by themselves. The clever cooks took subtle revenge by dumping all the leftovers into one dish after the food was chopped (*chop*) and shredded (*suey*). The miners liked it, and so have most Westerners ever since.

Seafood is the favorite fare for most people in Taiwan. It's available fresh daily, and there is enough to spare so that the island's fishermen earn about $400 million annually by exporting frozen seafood. With the climate so favorable in many parts of the island, fresh fruits and vegetables can be harvested year round.

Why is Chinese food so popular in cities around the world? It looks good and tastes good. This is achieved by careful preparation, quick cooking, and imaginative serving. Cooking and eating are important to the Chinese. Both dining out and banquets

A group of businessmen enjoy lunch in a restaurant.

are frequent occasions and are carefully planned. Usually Chinese meals are served at round tables at which the host sits with his back to the door and the guest of honor opposite him. Other guests are seated according to importance. Unlike many Western countries, in Taiwan the least important persons are seated to the right and left of the host. Not long ago, in a group of foreign dignitaries who were visiting Taipei, one self-important person complained: "Why am I sitting clear across the table from our host and our guides are sitting right next to him?"

Chopsticks are made of bamboo, wood, plastic, ivory, or silver. The Chinese place food on a revolving turntable located at the center of the table, so that several persons can make selections at the same time.

A waitress assembles snacks, called dim sum, on a cart. Inset: Seafood for sale in a market

Yum Cha, "Drink Tea," is somewhat comparable to high tea in Britain or coffee breaks in America. Cantonese-style snacks are offered in many Taiwan restaurants from breakfast time to 2 P.M. They are served from a wagon, rather like a dessert cart, where patrons can make their own choice. Dim sum, "snacks," are hot, cold, sweet, or salty. Popular dishes are white turnip cakes, fresh shrimp dumplings, and pastries made of rice.

Another popular sport played on grass is golf.

SPORTS AND RECREATION

Taiwan has almost any sport that exists in Western countries, including skiing, although the island is subtropical. In January and February there is enough snow for skiers at *Mt. Hohuan*, "Harmonious Happiness Mountain," in central Taiwan.

Grass skiing has grown in popularity. Nearly all of Taiwan's mountainous areas are perfect sites, and the weather is favorable most of the year. The sport was invented by a German and introduced to Taiwan in 1984. Participants in either snow or grass skiing wear tight suits to lessen wind resistance and use poles for balance. Both take part in competitions, observing the same rules. One major difference is the footwear—grass skiers wear boots that are fixed to caterpillar treads that have rollers. Part of the reason the sport has caught on in Taiwan is that the island is one of the world's major manufacturers of grass-skiing equipment.

Golf became a major sport in the 1990s. A Taipei headline

proclaimed, "Taiwan Goofy Over Golf." Taiwan is building more courses almost daily. There are approximately 400,000 golfers in Taiwan, and in 1990 there was only one course for every 14,000 players.

Other recreational activities include tennis, soccer, baseball (Taiwan's Little League teams have won six world championships), biking, camping, and mountain climbing.

The ocean is never far away in Taiwan. If the ocean is hard to reach, there are lakes, rivers, and streams to be used. Conventional sports such as swimming and fishing compete with new pleasures such as hang gliding, wind surfing, scuba diving, and underwater photography.

There also is cockfighting, considered a royal sport during the Tang Dynasty. It is a "sport" that has existed in Asia and elsewhere for centuries. Though it was outlawed in England in the 1800s, it did not totally disappear. It is condemned by many in Taiwan for its cruelty to animals, but it continues.

The martial arts go back more than two thousand years in Chinese heritage. Shadow boxing, *t'ai chi ch'uan*, has been around for a long time, but it is sometimes claimed that Kung Fu was invented by television and movies based on the practice. It is popular in Taiwan, as in Hong Kong and Chinese communities around the world. Karate, which originated in Asia, values graceful movements and rhythm. Before *karate*, which means "empty hand" in Japanese, emerged as a martial art, there was *shaolin chuan* boxing, which is taught by the marine corps in Taiwan and in private classes. It is intended for self-defense and also for beneficial exercise.

The Taiwan Adventist Hospital in Taipei

HEALTH

Although medical treatment and dental work cost far less in Taipei than in any Western country or in Japan, the quality of medical facilities and services is excellent and up to date. It is so good that medical tours organized in neighboring countries come to Taiwan for examination and treatment.

The use of herbal medicine began as far back as 3500 B.C. in China. An herbal doctor who lived during the Tang Dynasty insisted that rich and poor alike, not just emperors and their families and leading citizens, should receive equal treatment in his clinic. He emphasized the importance of a proper diet, and many Taiwan doctors follow his principles today. Currently there are insurance programs for about one-third of the people, but a comprehensive national health insurance program is scheduled for the near future.

Adults perform tai chi, *their morning exercise.*

There are many pharmacies in Taipei. Some specialize in "Western" medicine. Others feature only traditional Chinese pharmaceuticals, and some split the shop into two parts to offer both. There are one-man stands in the busy night market, sandwiched in among stalls that peddle clothing, appliances, food, and magazines. These stands are said to have fine restorative medications, some of which may be mixed by methods used in the Fukien Province on the mainland for nearly two centuries.

Acupuncture is an ancient Chinese form of needle therapy that sometimes cures or alleviates diseases that other treatment has failed to help. Its popularity has spread to Western countries.

Exercise is considered basic to good health and longevity. Early morning folk dancing is a popular activity in Taipei's New Park for residents who are middle-aged or older.

Chapter 8

RELIGION AND FESTIVALS

Dr. Sun Yat-sen, founding father of the Republic of China, regarded religion as one of the essential elements of human life. There is a Chinese saying: "It is better to believe in something than not to believe in anything." The Chinese believe in a variety of gods. Among the faiths in Taiwan are Buddhism, Taoism, Confucianism, Christianity, Islam, and folk religion.

FOLK RELIGION

The majority of Taiwanese are said to be followers of folk religion, which has rituals and theology intermingled with other forms of worship. Chinese immigrants to the island worshiped different gods because they came from different parts of the mainland and had various occupations. Carpenters, for example, had their own god, Lu Pam, who had been a famous carpenter in ancient China. Although most traditions have lasted for centuries, there have been some changes since 1950. Fewer people worship gods that are too specific. The waves of settlers in Taiwan's pioneer period brought their own god images and rituals to which they were accustomed on the mainland. In adapting old ways to the new environment, some changes occurred. New gods were even created. About two-thirds of the Taiwanese are followers of folk religion.

BUDDHISM

Buddhism was introduced to Taiwan in the late sixteenth century by Chinese believers, and has had much influence on Chinese folk religion. During the Japanese occupation various schools of Japanese Buddhism altered the standards that had been maintained by local Buddhists. Many religious leaders began to let their own strict ways slide; some married or ate meat, and the temples were decorated with mystic or Taoist paintings.

Sakyamuni Buddha, born in the sixth century B.C., was the son of a northern India Hindu king. Legend says that one day he left the palace where he had grown up in a protected environment and wandered among the people. He saw so much misery and misfortune that he began to doubt that Hinduism was the true religion. He finally gained his great enlightenment through long hours of sitting quietly in meditation. He came to feel that much suffering was due to ignorance and believed recovery could be gained from right living and mental discipline. Thus he became Buddha, the Enlightened One. Among Buddhist doctrines is the belief that all living creatures deserve mercy and must never be killed. Buddhists must be kind, charitable, and not seek help from others, but must look inward for self-improvement.

After Taiwan was returned to China at the end of World War II, many teachers came to restore discipline in the temple. Buddha and Kuan Yin, goddess of mercy, are the most famous gods in the

Left: A giant statue of Kuan Yin, goddess of mercy, stands on a hilltop overlooking Keelung Harbor. Above: The Taoist goddess of the sea, Matsu, holds the central place in a temple altar.

Buddhist tradition. Scholars and intellectuals were drawn to Buddhism. Most colleges in Taiwan have a Buddhist study group on campus. At present, about one million Taiwanese are Buddhists.

TAOISM

Taoism came to Taiwan toward the end of the Ming and beginning of the Ch'ing Dynasties. In the Chou Dynasty on the mainland, which was from 1122 to 249 B.C., the Taoist master Lao Tze worshiped nature and believed all things should be properly lined up with the earth. Where to build a house and where to place the door were important matters to ensure good fortune. Taoism holds that the heart must be free from desire and man should be "as serene as the ocean, as mobile as the wind." There are more than seven thousand Taoist temples and many more family Taoist shrines in Taiwan. The number of Taoist public buildings exceeds that of all other religions.

A portrait of Confucius

Taoism has long been viewed as an "original" Chinese religion, in contrast to Buddhism, Christianity, and Islam, all of which have foreign origins. It has close links to folk religion, and because of this it is frequently cited as the main religion of China. During the Japanese occupation of Taiwan, many Taoist temples and images were burned. Organized Taoism was revived in the middle of the twentieth century.

CONFUCIANISM

Confucianism, based on the teachings of the Chinese scholar and sage Confucius, is more an ethical code or code of honor than a religion or school of philosophy. Confucius, who lived from 555 to 479 B.C., had a group of disciples whom he taught to emphasize goodness in everyday life. The basic principle of Confucian ethics is *jen*, which has been translated into English as "human-heartedness," "benevolence," and "humanity."

In the Republic of China there is *ren-shing-wei*, "the flavor of human feeling," which makes feelings more important than facts in all relationships. Scholars have been searching for the reason why Confucianism seems an integral part of Taiwan's great energy and successful modernization. The innate courtesy, warmth, and geniality of the people in Taiwan make many visitors feel welcome.

CHRISTIANITY

The first Protestant missionaries came to Taiwan in 1627 from the Netherlands. They served the Dutch traders and made efforts to convert the nearest aborigines, but neglected the local Chinese. When the Manchus took over in 1638, the last missionaries were driven out. Centuries later, when the Communist party came into power on the mainland, religious freedom was suppressed, and many Chinese Christians fled to Taiwan. More than sixty denominations moved to the island. Today there are about 210,000 Presbyterians, 15,000 Baptists, and 5,500 Seventh-Day Adventists. Other congregations have smaller numbers.

Spanish missionaries brought Roman Catholicism to Taiwan, reaching Keelung and Tamsui in the north in 1626. The Dutch occupants of the island opposed attempts to found the Catholic Church, but in 1859 Spanish Dominicans from the Philippines managed to gain a foothold in Kaohsiung in southern Taiwan. Today there are about 292,000 Catholics in Taiwan, with some 800 priests of both Chinese and non-Chinese nationality.

ISLAM

Among the troops that Koxinga brought to Taiwan in the late Ming Dynasty were a number of Muslims. About twenty thousand Muslims came with the central government in 1949. The

An aboriginal bride and groom

development of Islam has been somewhat limited, but currently there are about fifty-nine thousand Muslims in the Taiwan area and five mosques.

RELIGION AMONG THE ABORIGINES

The Japanese colonists from the end of the nineteenth century to 1945 had forbidden the teaching of Christianity to the aborigines of Taiwan. After the island was returned to the Chinese, evangelism helped the Christian churches to grow. Since 1960 Christianity is dominant in the aborigine communities.

FESTIVALS

The greatest of all Chinese festivals is the Lunar New Year. The lunar calendar is the world's oldest calendar. On the first day of the first moon of the lunar calendar, a different creature begins a one-year reign in the recurring cycle of wild, domestic, or mythical creatures. The succession follows year after year in the same order. One year may be the Year of the Rat. The first month would be the rat, followed by lunar months of the ox, tiger, rabbit, dragon, snake, horse, sheep, monkey, chicken, dog, and pig. The next year would be the Year of the Ox, followed by lunar months of the tiger, rabbit, dragon, snake, horse, sheep, monkey, chicken, dog, pig, and rat, and so on. From ancient times the Chinese have believed that persons born in different years of the cycle possess certain characteristics. For example, 1992 was the Year of the Monkey. According to legend, those born in this year are clever, original, inventive, and able to solve problems with ease. But they also are inconsistent, cantankerous, troublesome, and love compliments. In addition they have fine memories, learn easily, are clever with money, and are held in high esteem.

The departure of the old year and arrival of the new always is accompanied by thousands of firecrackers meant to scare away evil spirits and invoke the gods' blessings.

The Lunar New Year, also known as the Spring Festival, is a joyous occasion for family reunions. It takes place in late January or February and the three-day holiday is a happy, noisy time with packed trains, planes, and buses bringing family members together. Some businesses remain closed for five days. Houses have been made spotless, and a great deal of food has been prepared for the celebrations.

The kitchen god, Tsao Chun, who has been represented all year by a colored print, usually hanging above the stove, makes his ascent heavenward a week before the New Year to give his report on family behavior to the Jade Emperor. Before his departure his lips have been daubed with something sweet to keep him quiet or to induce him to give a favorable report to the emperor. His departure is symbolized by burning his likeness along with plenty of paper money to give him a first-class round-trip. The kitchen god returns on New Year's Eve to an immaculate house, and a new drawing of him is placed on the wall. Once Tsao Chun is home again, the family enjoys a lavish feast in the hope that the table will be well-laden all year. Everyone wears his or her best clothes. Children are given red envelopes containing crisp new banknotes and are allowed to stay up late.

Because the Lunar New Year also serves as Spring Festival, the Chinese paste "spring couplets" around their doors—hoping for happiness in the coming year.

The Lantern Festival marks the end of the New Year celebrations in a brilliantly lit way. It arrives on the fifteenth day of the first moon. The Chinese used to believe they could see celestial spirits by the light of the first moon, so they lighted torches to improve visibility. Later lanterns were used, in a variety of beautiful and intricate shapes. The lanterns are either candle-lit or battery-powered. The festival has lantern processions and contests in which prizes are awarded for the best lanterns. Festival food has always been important. Yuan hsiao, associated with the lantern festivals, is a small dumpling made of rice and usually contains a sweet filling. The dumpling is round, symbolizing the full moon and complete family reunions.

Tomb-sweeping Day, an ancient holiday, also known as the Ching Ming Festival, takes place fifteen days after the spring equinox, about April 5. Families visit cemeteries to sweep the tombs of their ancestors, plant new trees, and bring fresh flowers. It is both a sorrowful occasion and a spring outing. The practice began in the Tang Dynasty in A.D. 618. A new coat of paint may be applied to the writing on the headstone. Then offerings of

Some traditional things associated with festivals are moon cakes, lanterns, and dragon boats.

flowers and other sacrificial items are placed on the grave and incense is burned.

The Dragon Boat Festival is a public holiday that features dragon boat races to commemorate the death of the poet-statesman, Chu Yuan, who drowned himself in a river in 299 B.C., hoping to call attention to the lack of government reforms. It also is observed as Poets' Day.

The story is told that the common people who revered Chu Yuan for his integrity rushed out in boats to search for him but failed. So they threw cooked rice into the river to kill the appetite of the fish who might otherwise nibble on the poet's body. From this came the custom still preserved today of serving *tsung-tsz,* rice dumplings wrapped in bamboo leaves and boiled, on Dragon Boat Day.

In Taiwan the dragon boats are about forty-two feet (thirteen meters) long. Twenty-two oarsmen sit two abreast and row to the beat of a drum handled by a crewman standing in the prow of the boat. Another crew member in the prow is there to snatch the flag at the finishing line. The pilot of each boat stands or sits astern. The Chinese welcome summer with the Dragon Boat Festival and look to the "dragon" to ensure rain for the crops.

The Month of Ghosts takes place during the seventh lunar month. The biggest occasion of the Month of Ghosts falls on the fifteenth day of the lunar month, some years in late July, but usually in August. The gates of the underworld are believed to open for the spirits to take a month-long vacation on earth. People burn symbolic money and incense and prepare food to appease the roaming spirits who are looking for a living body to inhabit. For more than fourteen hundred years the feast has been held in honor of the ghost, or *Chung Yuan*. On the eve of the celebration orange-red lanterns are hung out to light the path for the ghosts all over the island. To aid the spirits of those who drowned, miniature paper houses are set alight and launched on water to light the way to shore.

Today in Taiwan some people burn paper models of TV sets and luxury cars to show the spirits that the island's prosperity has not overlooked them. While many of today's Taiwanese no longer believe in the rituals, everyone is said to walk cautiously, and swimming loses some of its appeal during the month because of the countless frightful tales that have been handed down for generations. The spooky stories told are similar to those related in Western countries that observe Halloween.

Millions of people gather in open spaces to gaze at the moon during the Mid-Autumn (Moon) Festival, and they seem to find the moon more radiant than at any other season of the year. This corresponds to the harvest moon time in Western areas.

A legend says that Hou Yih was an officer in the emperor's bodyguard in China about 2000 B.C. He also was an expert archer. One day when ten suns appeared in the sky, threatening to scorch the earth, the emperor ordered Hou Yih to shoot nine of them. Hou Yih accomplished this with no difficulty, which so impressed the goddess of the western heavens that she asked him to build a palace of jade for her. He managed this brilliantly and was presented with a pill that would make him immortal, but with one condition. Hou Yih must undergo a year of prayer and fasting before he could swallow the magic pill. Hou Yih took the magic pill home and hid it.

Unfortunately, his beautiful wife, Chang-O, found the pill and promptly swallowed it. Immediately she was airborne, bound for eternal banishment on the moon. There she would enhance its radiance with her own beauty. Hou Yih set out in pursuit of his lovely but impetuous mate, but he was tossed back to earth by a typhoon. This story is told to every child on Taiwan as the Mid-Autumn, or Moon, Festival approaches. Another version of the legend holds that the unlucky young woman was so breathless on reaching the moon that she coughed and spit up the pill. It was transformed into a rabbit and Chang-O became a three-legged toad. This version may have been concocted to warn children not to take pills without being told to.

Double Tenth National Day commemorates the Wuchang Uprising on the mainland on October 10, 1911, which led to the establishment of the Republic of China on January 1, 1912. The

A dragon dance is performed on National Day.

president gives a public address in front of the Presidential
Building, followed by a parade of members from the armed forces
academies, various officeholders, folk dancers, and dragon
dancers. A brilliant display of fireworks over the Tamsui River
takes place at evening.

There are many other celebrations. The birthday of Kuan Yin,
goddess of mercy, is celebrated at Taipei's Lungshan Temple and
other temples in late March or early April, depending on the
lunar calendar. Also the birthday of Matsu, goddess of the sea, is
observed at hundreds of temples.

Chapter 9

ARTS AND CULTURE

LANGUAGE

More people speak Chinese as their native tongue than any other language in the world, but there are many dialects that are mutually difficult to understand. It is the only major modern writing system that uses ideograms, "idea pictures," written characters that depict ideas or objects. The oldest recorded ideographic symbols appeared on oracle ox bones and tortoise shells excavated in 1899 in Honan Province on the mainland. They are from the Shang Dynasty and are believed to date from about 1300 to 1028 B.C. They were consulted, for instance, to predict whether or not it would rain on a certain day. The writings were interpreted to answer yes or no.

Mandarin is the national language on both sides of the Formosa Strait. The spoken language has a tonal system, which means each syllable can be pronounced in four distinctive tones and each tone gives a new meaning to the word. In Taiwan the Mandarin dialect (guo-yu or kuo-yu) is based on the pronunciation that was used in the old imperial capital of Peking (now Beijing). It is the most melodious.

Shoppers watch an artist complete a painting at the Sunday flower and jade market in Taipei.

There is a local dialect called Taiwanese, derived from China's Fukien Province and commonly spoken in rural island communities. Some of Taiwan's older generation still speak Japanese, learned during the fifty years of Japanese occupation. English is a required subject for all Taiwanese students and is spoken by intellectuals, business executives, and professionals.

PAINTING

Painting is an integral part of Chinese culture. Chinese paintings are said to be easy to look at but hard to evaluate or describe, because the artists feel free to leave out objects not essential to their ideas. A fish may swim through water that is not shown; the flowing lines of the fish convey the spirit of movement, and the viewer's imagination fills in the rest. While

Chinese painting may tend toward impressionism, it is not abstract. Some realism is always there.

As in calligraphy, the artist must have an image of the finished work in his or her mind's eye–erasure, filling in, and painting over are forbidden. (This makes an artist's life more difficult, or at least more rigid, than a writer's, whose work may be edited by the writer or others a dozen times to get it right.)

In Taiwan basic painting equipment includes brushes, a cake of solidified ink, a stone slab on which the ink is ground and mixed with water, color pigments, and paper or silk. The brushes are usually of rabbit hair for delicate work, of sheep or goat hair for bolder strokes. Other brushes may be made from weasel, sable, fox, wolf, mouse whiskers, and even human baby hair.

During the Tang Dynasty painting flourished along with other intellectual and creative endeavors. Landscape art was developed. The artist Han Kan pleased Emperor Ming Huang with his paintings of horses.

Classical Chinese painting is still practiced in Taiwan. Colleges and universities have fine arts departments, and there are numerous art-related organizations. Lately many artists have pushed beyond the boundaries of the classical and combine elements that appeal to them from many traditions.

CALLIGRAPHY

To the Chinese, calligraphy is as much an art as painting. It must show originality, style, and personality. Its development into an art is attributed to the use of the Chinese writing brush and the paper, which is highly absorbent. The paper does not distort the figures while drying, nor can the writing be corrected. There

*A sculpture of
a crane in the
National Palace Museum.
To the Chinese,
the crane symbolizes
long life.*

are many styles of calligraphy. It is a major subject in Taiwan's schools from elementary to high school, and also in colleges.

The neighboring countries of Japan and Korea and several southeast Asia nations have made Chinese calligraphy a part of their own culture, and have developed their own schools and styles.

SCULPTURE

An earthenware statue of a female figure recently excavated on the mainland gives evidence that sculpture was a Chinese art in the Neolithic Age, more than 5,000 years ago. Shang Dynasty artists carved highly stylized animals in marble, with their surfaces decorated in patterns like those on bronzes of the same period. Buddhist sculpture flourished in the Tang period, from A.D. 618 to 907, but larger sculptures declined during the Ming and Ch'ing Dynasties, although jade, ivory, and wood carvings were excellent. It was not until the twentieth century that stone sculpture revived, with Western influence. The Taipei Art Exhibition Center has striking displays of modern Chinese sculpture, indoors and out. Today stainless steel also is being used for large sculptures.

BRONZES

The ancient Chinese people used rare bronze to cast ceremonial temple vessels, musical instruments, and weapons that were beautifully formed and elaborately decorated with inscribed Chinese characters. A world-famous bronze tripod, *Mao Kung Ting*, is on display at the National Palace Museum.

Beautiful bronzes are still found in Taiwan in temples, as statues at schools, and as decorative pieces in homes.

POTTERY AND PORCELAIN

The earliest prehistoric earthenwares were made of common clay. Later painted pottery was red-yellow based, with black and red patterns on the top. Black pottery was undecorated, and white pottery similar to porcelain was made sometime after the invention of written characters. Clay suitable for pottery making today is produced in Taipei County.

The Chinese probably were not the first to develop pottery for households and use at funerals. Egyptians used the potter's wheel before 4000 B.C., and other countries made excellent earthenware in early times. But only the Chinese produced wares so fine that the English called porcelains "chinaware."

Wholly decorative articles were rarely made. The Chinese insist on a functional use for their porcelains, earthenware, and stonewares. Fragments of water jars, food containers, and cooking pots have been found at the Yellow River sites where Chinese civilization began. Choice examples of the finest Chinese pottery of the last thousand years are now in museums all over the world. The best Chinese porcelains are considered priceless; some exist in private collections, but a few are on the market today.

OTHER FINE ART FORMS

Lacquer ware, textiles, and jade and ivory carvings show the flexibility of Chinese art. Lacquer was first used as a coating for bamboo furniture, possibly first introduced in southern China. Later it was found suitable for decorative objects. China was the first country to ornament its silken fabrics. Weaving and embroidery also are traced back to ancient times. Jade is one of the precious stones used for carving. In Taipei's National Palace, one of the most popular displays is the *fei-tsui*, a jade cabbage stalk carved during the Ch'ing Dynasty, from 1644 to 1911, complete with a camouflaged grasshopper.

Cloisonne enamel was made by a tedious hand process in Chinese courts for more than a thousand years. Cloisonne means "cell" or "partition." Flattened wires are attached to a metal base to form partitions, into which colored enamels (glass powder worked to a paste) are laid, fired, and polished to a lustrous finish.

ARCHITECTURE

Most of the very old buildings, found chiefly now in Taiwan's villages, are of Min-nan style from southern Fukien Province, built

Left: Artists paint vases in traditional designs.
Right: Cloisonne art is on display in the National Palace Museum.

by immigrants during the late Ming and Ching Dynasties about 1621 to 1895. The roofs of early houses were either "horseback," topped by a ridge that runs the entire length of the building, or "swallowtail," with the ends of the roofs curved upward like a bird's tail. Traditional Chinese houses were built in compounds with one or two courtyards within the walled perimeter.

The ridges and beams of a house were usually carved in ornamental designs pertaining to water, such as ripples, seaweed, fish, and dragons, believed to prevent fire. There are many traditional-style residences in Taiwan, but most are variations of a three-sectioned compound, a central building with two perpendicular wings.

Despite the many religions most temples have the same basic structure. There are more than five thousand temples that have some particular architectural significance.

During the past decade Taiwan has had a building boom both

in the cities and in the rural areas. Many commercial buildings are box-shaped with extensive use of glass, as in many cities around the world. Large government-sponsored projects and public buildings copy traditional forms, usually following models of the late Ming and Ching Dynasties. Some try to adapt the old to the new in a distinctive Chinese style that lends a Chinese "flavor" to modern convenience.

CHINESE OPERA

Chinese opera has many regional forms. In Taiwan, Peking Opera is performed on stage and television. Its origins are usually traced back to regional theater companies that gathered in Peking in 1790 to celebrate the emperor's birthday. Many companies stayed on after the festivities were ended and gave performances for the general public. It is still appreciated in Taiwan but it has to compete these days with videos and television. Most young people, it is said, are interested only in westernized pop songs.

Chinese opera is unique. The music sounds jangling to Western ears, and the falsetto voices used in dialogue and song are not in the normal speech range.

The stylized acting also takes training and years to master. Stage props are minimal, often consisting only of a carpet, two wooden chairs, a small table, and a plain backdrop. The orchestra sits in an area of the stage to the right of the audience. Percussion, string, and wind instruments are used, playing simple, repetitious melodies.

The costumes are gorgeous silks and satins, elaborately embroidered. Headgear is intricate, widely varied, and indicates the rank of the person portrayed. Colors used artfully in masks

An operatic performance

and face paint symbolize different human gifts and qualities: red for loyalty, black for integrity, white for power or treachery.

There are eighteen kinds of beards. Each beard has a meaning: a purple beard, for example, usually means a famous general. Only young scholars or lovers are beardless.

Chinese opera contains stylized pantomime, martial arts, and *kuo chu*, ingenious acrobatics. The plots, drawn from popular novels, historical events, folklore, and mythology, are easy to follow. Because of this, it is not necessary for the audience to understand the language to enjoy the performance.

CHINESE MUSIC

Many Chinese schools have youth orchestras and bands that give public performances, using both traditional and modern

*A young girl plays bells during a ceremony
in the Confucian temple in Taipei.*

instruments. Taiwan has produced numerous musicians considered world class. Western classical music is regularly performed by the Taiwan Provincial Symphony Orchestra and Taipei's Municipal Symphony Orchestra. Traditional music stems from special temple rites and from folk music.

OTHER PERFORMING ARTS

Modern dance has gained in popularity in the last decade. Some dances combine Chinese and Western styles. Some of the liveliest song-and-dance shows are performed at the aborigine villages where the costumes are vividly colored and decorated, and the headdresses that adorn aborigine girls are bright with beads, tassels, and feathers. The young men also are brilliantly costumed, often with wrap-around fringed skirts.

Feature-length color movies were made in Taiwan in 1960, a few years earlier than in either Hong Kong or on the mainland. In

Lion dancers

1980 the film business faced competition from MTV's, centers with rooms for individual viewing of videotapes. But a new wave of filmmakers took over, and in 1988 more than three hundred Chinese language motion pictures were approved for screening by the government. Most were produced locally, but some were made in Hong Kong. The Government Information Office established a special foundation and allocated millions to be used in making better films.

It is said that the Taiwanese view more movies per resident each year than any other country in the world, including America.

FOLK ARTS

Folk arts are a major part of life events such as births, birthdays, marriages, and death. Two of the most popular folk art performances are the dragon dance and the lion dance, a part of all important celebrations.

The Chinese revere the dragon, which symbolizes power, dignity, and good luck. When the dragon dance is performed at night, someone carries a flaming torch to illuminate the procession. It also is performed in the daytime when the many colors of the dragon's head and body glitter in the sunlight.

The lion dance, which requires fewer participants, is performed more often in smaller dance areas. One person manipulates the head and one the tail. Sometimes a third person wearing the mask of the laughing Buddha leads and teases the lion into action.

Many other performances and games go back thousands of years, such as shuttlecock kicking, jumping rope, and spinning tops. Faced with the plastic age in toys, many traditional folk games are in danger of disappearing. The government is making special efforts to preserve traditional Chinese folk arts in Taiwan.

HANDICRAFTS

Two of the most popular handicraft arts are puppets and paper cutting. Chinese hand puppetry, shadow puppetry, and marionettes are ancient folk arts. The hand puppets are elaborately dressed and wear symbolic face paint. Shadow puppetry is performed in the dark with shadows projected on a white screen or cloth by bright lights. Marionettes include string-suspended puppets, walking string puppets, and stick puppets. String-suspended puppets, the most popular, are brought to life by a performer who uses ten control strings.

Paper cutting has been a favorite diversion among Chinese women for years. The cutouts are widely used at holidays, when they may be very intricate. For ordinary days, women favor

Left: Traditional wooden toys are in danger of disappearing in this age of plastic toys.   Right: Eighty-four-year-old puppet master Li Tien Lu poses with his puppets in 1993.

flowers, birds, pets, and farm animals. The subjects are unlimited, and gifted paper cutters can present whole stories or operas in their designs.

At present, city and county culture centers throughout Taiwan are planning a number of museums featuring exhibits of local folk art. Among the many exhibitions there undoubtedly will be many fine examples of macrame (knot work) and decorative tassels made from tiny knots. The art of knot tying goes back to imperial days when Chinese maidens did embroidery and knot work using colorful pieces of leftover fabrics. Beautiful baskets are fashioned from bamboo and rattan, and so are elegant lamps. All of Taiwan's diverse handicrafts take agile fingers, concentration, and often years of study.

A small plot of land grows rice, vegetables, and flowers.

Chapter 10

BUSY NATION, BOUNTIFUL LAND

AGRICULTURE

In the late 1980s, cultivated land made up about a quarter of Taiwan's land surface, and the number of agricultural workers was about 14 percent of the work force. Farmers used tons of chemical fertilizers, animal feed, and pesticides, and spent about 200 million Taiwan dollars on livestock medication and chemicals.

Because of the warm, wet climate, crops are subject to frequent damage from disease and insects, as well as from seasonal typhoons. As in other industrialized countries, farming, once a major factor in Taiwan's economy, is struggling to survive. The government has begun programs to improve rural living, hoping to keep the farmers on the farms instead of seeking better incomes in the city.

In Taiwan a change in diet has resulted from the reduction of rice and sugarcane acreage to make room for feed grain. Fruit and flowers, which have high value in today's market, have become more common. Dairy farming retains government support, while beef farming has been cut back. Poultry exports are expanded, but

Yang Ming Park in Taipei

fisheries are the main source of animal protein. Through the improvement in fishing gear and vessels, deep sea fishing has been increased. The government is teaching farmers better marketing methods, and many small farms have been consolidated for more efficient results.

ONE BIG BOTANICAL GARDEN

One of the Chinese arts is creating beautiful gardens. Outside the busiest commercial areas, Taiwan is one big botanical garden. Like Japan and other countries, Taiwan has to conserve space. Small areas are cultivated and give an impression of spaciousness

Beach morning glories

through blending shrubbery and flowers with ponds, rock gardens, grottoes, and little decorative bridges.

The mountains offer a panorama of vegetation, greenery, and blooms, with habitats from the tropical through the subtropical to colder zones. A variety of plants thrive in various environments, and particularly rare tropical flowers are found on the Hengshu Peninsula at the southern tip of the island. Even the sandy beaches and rocky coastline have plants with overlapping leaves to resist sand and strong winds while retaining moisture. Beach morning glories are found in otherwise barren areas where nothing else can survive. Their roots are stewed and used to treat rheumatism and arthritis.

There are 4,000 species of vascular plants (those which have vessels or ducts to carry fluids). This includes 366 native species of orchids. At Yangmingshan National Park, just outside Taipei, is the largest orchid farm in Asia. When it's cherry blossom time in Yangmingshan, police control is often needed for the crowds who flock to enjoy the flowers and perfumed breezes. The trees have clusters of tiny flowers; the Japanese strain is white, the variety native to Taiwan is rose-colored.

St. John's Lily, called the *wenchu* orchid, although it does not belong to the orchid family, blooms in the summer with leaves as lovely as its flowers. It grows in gardens and parks, on campuses, and even on traffic islands. Its root is often used to relieve insect bites. When the first spring rains fall, farmers start planting the lotus. Its pink buds rise from among green umbrellalike leaves and are often a subject for painters and poets. A versatile plant, its rootstock makes a flavorful dish, the seeds are served as dessert, and the seed hearts are used in herbal medicines.

TREES

Though more than half the island is tree-covered and there are more than two hundred different commercial species of trees, the government has found it important to plan reforestation and severely punish those who engage in illegal lumbering activities. There also is a plan to save venerable trees. At least 842 are more than a century old. The 300 oldest will be protected under law as a part of the cultural heritage.

FRUITS

Over the centuries many nonindigenous fruits were brought to Taiwan by immigrants. Bananas, pineapples, papayas, and guavas were introduced in the seventeenth century; pears and ponkas (mandarin oranges) came in the eighteenth. Among newly introduced exotic fruits are "wax" apples that may be eaten raw, canned, pickled, or made into juice. Passion fruit, which originated in Brazil's rain forest, usually is grown in plantations on the slopes of hills, and is made into canned juice or frozen for export. Citrus fruit, bananas, and pineapples are most profitable; more than a million tons are exported annually.

A barking deer (left) and the Chinese leopard (right)

ANIMALS

Livestock raising is an important economic factor in Taiwan. Hogs are raised for local consumers, and the meat is frozen for export. Cattle, sheep, rabbits, and poultry are also produced. Geese are raised for eggs as well as roasting.

Taiwan has a variety of wild and exotic animals. The Formosan macaque (a form of monkey) is the only nonhuman primate found on the island. Its ancestors migrated from the mainland about forty-five thousand years ago. The tiny barking deer (muntjac) is very shy and seldom seen. Other animals include the Formosan black bear; the Chinese leopard, commonly called the "stone tiger"; the Chinese civet, known as the "pen cat" because its fur is used in calligraphy brushes; the crab-eating mongoose; and the Formosan flying fox, the largest bat on Taiwan.

The stock exchange in Taipei

THE ECONOMIC MIRACLE

Taiwan owes its amazing prosperity to the fact that its wide variety of exports finds customers all over the world. Manufactured goods now make up the bulk of these exports, but agriculture and the fishing industry also contribute to Taiwan's "economic miracle." When the central government moved to Taiwan at the end of 1949, the outlook was anything but bright. But the relatively new nation surprised the world by its economic development in some forty years.

Foreign trade and wise investments have helped a poor, undeveloped country to become an affluent, progressive one without creating a huge gap between rich and poor. Other achievements have been sound financial administration, the maintenance of stable commodity prices with little inflation, an exceptionally low unemployment rate, and a world-record-breaking rate of savings.

Sungshan domestic airport terminal building in Taipei

TRANSPORTATION

In recent years the government has completed a number of major transportation projects, including a mass rapid transit system in Taipei, more freeways and cross-island highways, and a round-the-island railway system. The overall policy is to increase safety, convenience, and comfort and to cut down travel time.

Taiwan's first "bullet" train is under construction. At an estimated speed capacity of 217 miles per hour (349 kilometers per hour) it will equal the fastest French trains and exceed both Germany's and Japan's bullet trains.

There are two international airports, Chiang Kai-shek in Taoyuan in northern Taiwan and Hsiaokang in Kaohsiung in the south; and there are a number of domestic terminals.

Water transportation is of vital importance in trade-oriented Taiwan. A great amount of freight is handled at island ports. There are four international harbors—Keelung, Kaohsiung, Hualien, and Taichung—and Suao harbor, which serves as a supplementary port to Keelung. Wharves and storage facilities have been expanded; cargo-handling equipment has been greatly improved to handle the booming foreign trade. Car ferries and boats offer daily service to and from points on the scenic east coast or the Pescadores.

Taxis and buses are plentiful in Taipei. The mass rapid transit system has helped to ease some of the congestion, but Taipei traffic remains comparable to Rome, New York, and Mexico City in rush hour. A fleet of deluxe highway express buses uses the north/south expressway between major cities.

INDUSTRY

Over the past four decades, industrial development has created a gross national product exceeding $171 billion and foreign exchange reserves surpassing $70 billion, both in U.S. dollars. Although Taiwan is a small country without natural resources such as crude oil and coal, it has been pointed out by a national observer that Taiwan has a rich reserve of brains to dispense.

Manufacturers are emphasizing quality, reliability, and the creation of new products. For example, the Industrial Technology Research Institute has developed Taiwan's first WORM (for "write once, read many") computer optical disk drive. The WORM is for information that is to be saved without alteration, such as contracts, transaction records, and library cataloging. The device

Some common environmental problems faced by industrial nations are the careless dumping of litter and garbage (left) and air pollution (right).

can access graphics and photographic material in just 150 milliseconds.

The environmental problems of rapid growth are a major concern of the government. A visiting environmentalist recently observed that there are more cellular phones per capita than anywhere else in the world, and he warned that without an all-out cleanup of air, water, and coastal waters, the people of Taiwan would soon find themselves with more cellular phones than air to breathe or water to drink.

The government is aware that in the past production was the main aim, with little attention paid to the deteriorating environment, but it is now taking steps so that the country can continue to move forward without sacrificing the beautiful land that was *"Ihla formosa."*

Chapter 11

TAIWAN TODAY: MARCH TOWARD DEMOCRACY

contributed by Parris H. Chang, Ph.D.

The lifting of the thirty-eight-year-old martial law in July 1987–the end of emergency rule–by Chiang Ching-kuo marked an important milestone in Taiwan's progress toward democracy. It not only legally permitted the establishment of the Democratic Progression party (DPP) and other opposition parties but it also expanded the freedoms of the press and of the assembly, and it enormously enhanced popular political participation.

The death of President Chiang Ching-kuo in January 1988, who was instrumental in launching Taiwan's political reforms, did not disrupt the reform movement. In fact, the pace of Taiwan's political liberalization and democratization has been accelerated since President Lee Teng-hui took over the leadership of the Kuomintang (KMT) regime.

TAIWAN'S REFORM UNDER LEE TENG-HUI

President Lee is a native of Taiwan; he was educated in Taiwan, Japan, and the United States. He received his Ph.D. in economics

Protestors demonstrated in 1989 against a bill that would allow aged legislators to receive generous pensions on retirement.

from Cornell University in 1968. Before Lee entered government service in 1972, he was a professor of economics. In his political career Lee has held the posts of mayor of Taipei, governor of Taiwan, and vice-president of the Republic of China. As a native son, Lee has intimate and detailed knowledge of Taiwan and fully understands the Taiwanese people's feelings and aspirations. He is a man of the world—extremely well-informed about international affairs. Most important of all, he is a man of vision and a democrat. He is genuinely committed to a system of constitutional democracy in Taiwan and has sponsored reform measures to that effect.

One of these measures was to end the terms of the senior members of three parliamentarian bodies, the Legislative Yuan, the National Assembly, and the Control Yuan, by December 31, 1991. These aging mainlander politicians were elected before 1947 and remained in office, without reelection, for over forty years. These

parliamentarians claimed the KMT government was the
government of all of China; therefore, they should be allowed to
serve indefinitely.

In June-July 1990 President Lee convened a forum called the
National Affairs Conference (NAC), which brought together
approximately 150 politicians, academics, businesspeople, and
opinion leaders. Among them were leaders of the DPP, dissidents,
and several Taiwan experts from the United States. The members
discussed the state of the nation and offered recommendations on
constitutional revisions and democratic change. Although the NAC
was not meant to be a constitutional convention, there was a
broad consensus among most of the participants on both the
direction and the agenda of future reform. One of the major issues
agreed on at the forum was direct election of the future president
by the people.

Over the years, the KMT regime's preoccupation with
Communist subversion, the political opposition of the native
Taiwanese, and the tendency of the security apparatus to abuse its
power has impeded respect for human rights and the growth of a
genuine democratic system embodied in the constitution of the
Republic of China (ROC). President Lee announced on April 30,
1991, the end of any remaining restrictions on freedoms of press,
speech, assembly, and other political rights. This meant the
president would no longer wield enormous powers. It was the
beginning of a more democratic system on Taiwan. It also
signaled Taipei's friendly gesture across the Formosa Strait, an
abandonment of the KMT claim to be the sole legitimate
government of China, and a desire to coexist peacefully with the
Communist regime.

Left: In 1990 students spray painted slogans calling for democratic reform on the Chiang Kai-shek Memorial. Above: President Lee Teng-hui smiles as he tells reporters he will go to Beijing, China, if he is invited as president of the Republic of China.

However, Beijing has not reciprocated and still refuses to renounce the use of force in solving its relations with Taiwan. To the Communist rulers in China, the KMT has lost the civil war, the Nationalist government should be taken over, and Taiwan should be reunited with China, and made a provincial unit, like Hong Kong.

WHO'S AFRAID OF DEMOCRACY?

Opposition to change does exist within the KMT despite popular demands for democratic reform and President Lee Tanghui's commitment to pursue democracy. Democracy entails the redistribution of power and resources. Conservatives, the KMT parliamentarians and their followers, and some vested interests have tried to block or slow down many of the reforms.

The question of who, the president or the premier, should have the ultimate authority and how they should be selected are major political issues that remain to be settled. Thus far, most Taiwanese favor a presidential system and support the direct, popular election of the president. Their two strongest arguments are (1) Taiwan needs a strong leader, and (2) direct, popular election of the president underscores the democratic principle of the "consent of the governed."

On the other hand, many mainlander politicians favor a parliamentary or cabinet system and call for indirect election of the president by the National Assembly. Their rationale is that if a president is elected by the 20 million people in Taiwan, he is only president of Taiwan, not China. They argue that the president of the ROC should be elected by the National Assembly, which consists of national "members at large" representing the mainland and overseas Chinese constituencies (even though they would be elected only by voters in Taiwan). In reality, many mainlander politicians in the KMT simply do not want a president who will exercise real power and who is sure to be a native Taiwanese.

Exactly how the president will be elected, how relations will evolve between the president and the premier and between the executive and the legislative branches, and other major constitutional issues will be worked out by a special session of the National Assembly in March 1994. Three hundred twenty-five new National Assembly members have been elected by voters. They will write a new constitution or amend the ROC constitution, which was adopted in 1947 when Chiang Kai-shek was in office.

STEPS TOWARD DEMOCRACY

Taiwan has come a long way, and much progress has been made. Now that martial law has been lifted and opposition parties can legally compete, the overall political processes are relatively open. There is greater freedom of expression, as the authorities now tolerate the opposition that is openly advocating Taiwan's independent nationhood and separation from China.

Consequently, Taiwan's influence in the world has been growing. Its political reforms have captured worldwide attention. The contrast between Taiwan's transition from an authoritarian one-party system to a multiparty competitive, democratic system and China's suppression of the pro-democracy movement is striking. Because of these reforms, Taiwan has improved its international image markedly and gained more respect. However, Taiwan is still not a member of the UN because the People's Republic of China (PRC) claims that it is a province of China, and the PRC enjoys veto power in the UN Security Council.

The DPP, the major opposition party, is challenging the KMT for power. Composed primarily of natives of Taiwan, it is gaining increasing popular support among the farmers, middle class, and workers. In the legislative elections in December 1992, the DPP won 52 seats (to 102 for the KMT) in the 161-member Legislative Yuan. Many observers predict that the DPP could capture control of the government before the end of the twentieth century.

Young Taiwanese citizens

THE FUTURE

People in Taiwan want democracy. If the New World Order is "a growing community of democracies anchoring international peace and stability, and a dynamic free-market system generating prosperity and progress on a global scale," as defined by former United States President George Bush, then Taiwan is a part of this new order and can contribute much to its expansion and consolidation. Taiwan does have a thriving market economy, and it is making rapid progress toward becoming a true democracy.

Since 1979 the United States has switched diplomatic recognition from the ROC in Taiwan to the PRC in Beijing and maintained only "nongovernmental" relations with the people of Taiwan. On the other hand, the U.S. Congress has passed the "Taiwan Relations Act," which provides a protective umbrella over Taiwan, including sales of sufficient defensive weapons to safeguard against invasion or threat of force by the Communists. The special relationship between the United States and Taiwan has forestalled Beijing's possible use of force and enabled Taiwan to pursue economic modernization and implement democratic reform.

Relatives of victims, killed by Nationalist Chinese troops during a demonstration in 1947, commemorate the event.

MAP KEY

Place	Grid
Anp'ing	C3
Bashi Channel	E3, E4
Changhua	B3
Ch'angpin	C4
Ch'aochou	D3
Ch'ech'eng	D3
Ch'hsing Yen (islands)	E3
Chianan	D3
Chiahsien	C3
Chiai (Chiayi)	C3
Chiali	C3
Chiaoch'i	B4
Chiaopanshan	B4
Chiapaot'ai	B4
Chichi	C3
Chihpen	D4
Ch'ihshang	C4
Ch'ihtung	D3
Ch'ihu	C3
Ch'iku	C3
Chilung (Keelung)	A4
Ch'ingshui	B3
Chinkuashih	A4
Chinmen	B1
Chinshan	A4
Chinshui	B3
Chipei Tao (island)	C2
Chip'ing	C3
Ch'ishan	D3
Choshui Ch'i (river)	B4, C3, C4
Chunan	B3
Chungli	B4
Chungliao	D4
Chungp'u	C3
Chungyang Shanmo (mountain range)	B4, C3, C4, D3
Chushan	C3
Chutung	B4
Erhlin	C3
Erhshui	C3
Fangliao	D3
Fangshan	D3
Fenglin	C4
Fengpin	C4
Formosa Strait	A3, B2, B3, C1, C2
Fukuei Chiao	A4
Fuli	C4
Haian Shanmo (mountain range)	C4
Han	B4
Hengch'un	D3
Houlung	B3
Hsiaohungt'ou Hsu (island)	E4
Hsia-tan-shui Ch'i (river)	C3, D3
Hsichi Hsu (island)	C2
Hsijehweng Shan (peak)	B4
Hsilo	C3
Hsilo Ch'i (river)	C3
Hsinch'eng	B4
Hsinchu	B3
Hsinhua	C3
Hsinshih	C3
Hsintien	B4
Hsip'ing Hsu (island)	C2
Hsiukuluan Ch'i (river)	C4
Hsiyu	C2
Hsuehchia	C3
Hua Hsu (island)	C2
Hualien	C4
Hualien Ch'i (river)	C4
Huap'ing Hsu (island)	A4
Huhsi	C2
Hungf'ou Hsu (island)	D4
Hungmao	B3
Huoshao Tao (island)	D4
Huoshaoliao	A4, B4
Huwei	C3
Ilan Ch'uan (river)	B4
Jenli	C3
Jihyueht'an	C3
Juisui	C4
Kangshan	D3
Kaohsiung	D3
Kaohsiunghsien	D3
K'ouhu	C3
Kuan Shan (peak)	C3
Kuanhsi	B4
Kuanmiao	D3
Kuanshan	C4
Kuanyin	A4
Kueishan Tao (island)	B4
Kunghsi	B4
Kuohsing	B3
Laohuk'ou	B4
Lichiang	D3
Linyuan	D3
Liuch'iu Hsu (island)	D3
Liuch'iut'ai	C3
Lotung	B4
Luchiang	B3
Luyeh	D4
Mailiao	C3
Mao Hsu (island)	C2
Matou	C3
Meinung	D3
Miaoli	B3
Mienhua Hsu (island)	A4
Nan Wan	E3
Nanao	B4
Nanchuang	B3, B4
Nanhsi	C3
Nanhuta Shan (peak)	B4
Nant'ou	C3
Niujouch'i	C3
Oluan Pi (cape)	E3
Pacific Ocean	B4, C4, D3, D4, E4
Paiho	C3
Paisha	C2
Pat'ung Kuan	C4
Peichiang	C3
Peichiang Ch'i (river)	C3
Peinan	D4
Peinanta Ch'i (river)	C4, D4
Peit'ou	A4
P'engchia Hsu (island)	A4
P'enghu	C2
P'enghu Shuitao	C2, C3
Pescadores (islands)	C2
P'ingtung	D3
P'otzu	C3
Puli	C3
Putai	C3
Quemoy (island)	B1
Sanch'a	B3
Sanchih	A4
Sanch'ung (Shanchung)	A4
Sanhsient'ai	C4
Sanhsing	B4
Santiao Chiao	A4, B4
Shamei	B1
Shoufeng	C4
South China Sea	C1, C2, C3, D1, D2, D3, E1, E2, E3
Ssuch'ungch'i	D3
Suao	B4
Ta Hsu (island)	C2
Taan Ch'i (river)	B3, B4
Tach'i	B4
Tachia	B3
Tachia Ch'i (river)	B3, B4
Tachoshui	B4
Tahu	B3
T'aichung (Taichung)	B3
T'aichunghsien	B3
T'aihsi	C3
T'aima	D3, D4
T'ainan	C3, D3
T'ainanhsien	C3
Taipei	A4
T'aipei-hsien	A4, B4
T'aip'ing Shan (mountain range)	B4
T'aitung	D4
Tanshui (Tamsui)	A4
Tanshui Ho (river)	A4, B4
T'aosai	B4
T'aoyuan	B4
Tapanlieh	E3
Tatelu	D3
Tatu Ch'i (river)	B3, B4, C3
Tat'un Shan (peak)	A4
Tatzuli Ch'i (river)	B4
Tawu	D3
Tayuan	A4
Tinghuanghsi	A4
T'ouch'eng	B4
Tounan	C3
Ts'aot'un	C3
Ts'engwen Ch'i (river)	C3
Tsoying	D3
T'uch'ang	B4
Tungchi Hsu (island)	C2
Tungchiang	D3
Tungho	D4
Tungshih	B3
Tungting Hsu (island)	B1
Wuch'i	B4
Wuch'iu Hsu (island)	A2
Wulai	B4
Wushe	B4
Yenshui	C3
Yu Shan (peak)	C3
Yuanli	B3
Yuanlin	C3
Yuli	C4
Yunlin	C3
Yuweng Tao (island)	C2

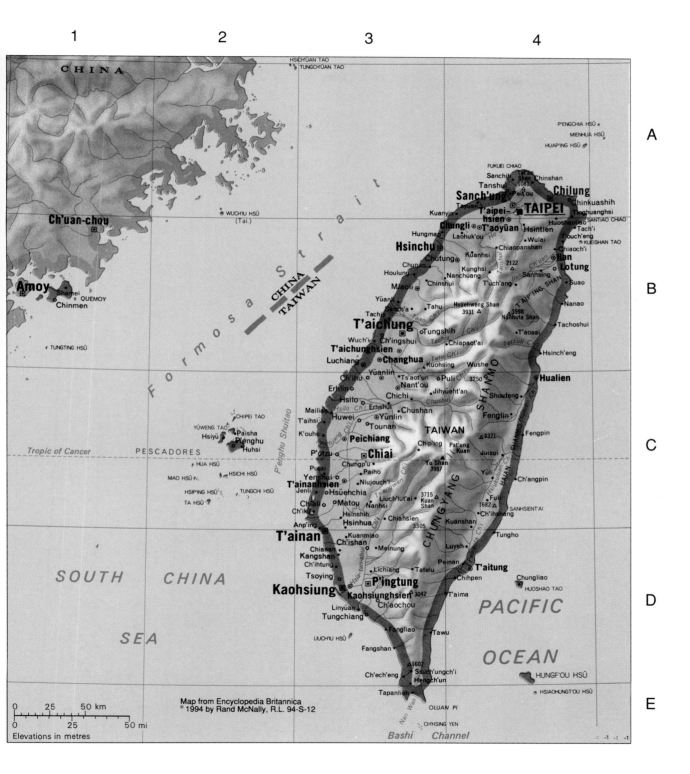

Map from Encyclopedia Britannica
© 1994 by Rand McNally, R.L. 94-S-12

MINI-FACTS AT A GLANCE

GENERAL INFORMATION

Official Name: The Republic of China, *Chung-hua Min-Kuo*

Capital: Taipei

Government: Taiwan is a multi-party republic. The president is the chief of state and the premier is the head of government. The president is elected by the National Assembly for a six-year term. In the spring of 1994, the National Assembly amended the constitution to shorten the term to four years and granted the citizens in Taiwan the right to elect the president. There are five yuans (governing bodies): the 161-member law-making Legislative Yuan (parliament) to which the Executive Yuan (Council of Ministers) is responsible, the Control Yuan, the Judicial Yuan, and the Examination Yuan. The president appoints a premier to head the Executive Yuan. In the past decade Taiwan has seen a transition from an authoritarian one-party system to a multi-party competitive democratic system. Taiwanese citizens over age 20 can vote in elections.

For administrative purposes Taiwan is divided into 16 counties and five municipalities, plus Taipei and Kaohsiung municipalities which have the status of province.

Religion: The constitution does not support any religion but guarantees freedom of religion for all. Almost one-half of the Taiwanese practice Buddhism; the rest practice Taoism, Confucianism, Christianity (chief denominations are Roman Catholic, Presbyterian, Baptist, and Seventh-Day Adventist), and folk religion.

Taiwanese believe in a variety of gods such as *Matsu*, goddess of the sea; *Kuan Yin*, goddess of mercy; *Lu Pam*, god of carpenters; and *Tsao Chun*, god of the kitchen. There are more than 7,000 Taoist temples and numerous Buddhist shrines in Taiwan. Confucianism is an integral part of Taiwan's great energy and successful modernization; it has influenced Chinese people in ethics, morality, and academic thinking.

Language: Mandarin Chinese is the official language. Chinese is the only major modern writing system that uses ideograms, "idea pictures." The spoken Mandarin has a tonal system with four distinctive tones to pronounce each syllable, which gives a new meaning to the word. The Taiwanese dialect of Chinese is spoken in rural communities. Some older Taiwanese still speak Japanese. English is a required subject for all students.

National Flag: The present flag was adopted in 1895 by Sun Yat-sen as the Nationalist (Kuomintang or KMT) party flag. In 1914 a red field was added and in 1928 this flag was adopted as the national flag of China by the Nationalists and remains in use in Taiwan.

The flag is red with a blue field in the upper-left quadrant. A 12-pointed white sun, known as the white sun in the blue sky, appears on the blue field. The 12 points of the sun represent the 12 two-hour periods of the day. The red, white, and blue colors represent the spirit of liberty, fraternity, and equality, respectively.

Money: The New Taiwan dollar (NT$) is the official currency. In spring 1994 one NT$ was worth $0.03 in United States currency.

Membership in International Organizations: Taiwan is a member of Asian Development Bank (ADB) and Asia-Pacific Economic Cooperation (APEC). Taiwan was granted observer status at the General Agreement on Tariffs and Trade (GATT) in 1992, and expects to become a full member in 1995.

Weights and Measures: The metric system is in use. Some local measures such as *catty* (1.1 lb.), *li* (0.31 mi.), *ch'ih* (1.09 ft.), and *chia* (2.39 acres) are still in use.

Population: 1994 estimate, 21,299,000; 1,533 persons per sq. mi. (592 persons per sq km); 75 percent urban, 25 percent rural.

Cities:

Taipei	2,718,000
Kaohsiung	1,396,000
Taichung	774,000
T'ainan	690,000
Panchiao	543,000

(Population based on 1991 estimates.)

GEOGRAPHY

Coastline: 555 mi. (893 km)

Highest Point: Yu Shan at 13,113 ft. (3,997 km); also known as Jade Mountain and Mt. Morrison.

Lowest Point: Sea level

Rivers and Lakes: Most of the rivers originate in the east-central highlands and have short courses. Tamsui, Hsintien, and Keelung (or Chilung) are the major rivers. The Chosui River draining westward is the longest river (114 mi.; 183 km). Sun Moon Lake is situated in the central highlands at 2,415 ft. (736 m). Alluvial soil on the plains and river valleys cover about one-fourth of the island.

Forests: Some 60 percent of the land is under forests and about 200 different commercial species of trees exist in Taiwan. Mangrove forests are found in the tidal basins and coastal areas. The chief trees are ficua, pandanus, palm, teak, bamboo, rattan, cedar, oak, camphor, cypress, pine, spruce, juniper, and hemlock; forest products include plywood, paper, camphor, bamboo, and wood. There are some 366 native species of orchids. The Yangmingshan National Park has the biggest orchid farm in Asia. The Taiwanese government promotes reforestation extensively.

Taroko Gorge has been made a national park to preserve its natural beauty. The *Kenting*, "Plowmen," National Park is in the Hengchun Peninsula in the south; it is Taiwan's first national park intended to preserve and protect the marine and land wonders of the area. The Alishan Forest Recreational Area is a popular resort.

Wildlife: Taiwan's varied wildlife includes the Formosan macaque (monkey), the tiny barking deer, the Formosan black bear, monkeys, wild boars, Chinese leopards, civets, mongeese, gibbons, flying squirrels, and flying foxes. Birds include pheasants, geese, flycatchers, kingfishers, larks, and many other species. The Yu Shan National Park is a wildlife preserve.

Climate: The subtropical monsoon climate has warm and humid summers lasting from May until September. Average temperatures are just under 71° F (22° C) in the north and 76° F (24° C) in the south. Mild winter lasts from December till February; frost and snow occasionally occur at elevations above 4,000 ft. (1,219 m). Summer storms often bring heavy rainfall; typhoons (tropical cyclones) usually strike in July, August, and September. The average rainfall is 100 in. (254 cm); Keelung is one of the wettest cities with an average of 214 days of rainfall.

Greatest Distance: North to South: 235 mi. (378 km)
East to West: 90 mi. (145 km)

Area: 13,900 sq. mi. (35,000 sq km) including the Pescadores Islands

ECONOMY AND INDUSTRY

Agriculture: About one-fourth of Taiwan's land is under cultivation. The chief crops are rice, maize, tea, tobacco, groundnuts, cassava, sweet potatoes, sugarcane, and vegetables. Tropical and citrus fruits grown are pineapples, guava, pears, mandarin oranges, wax apples, passion fruit, oranges, papayas, watermelons, and bananas. Chemical fertilizers and pesticides are used heavily. Rice and sugarcane cultivation is decreasing and being replaced by feed grain, fruit, flower, and dairy farming. Hogs, cattle, sheep, rabbits, ducks, geese, and chickens are raised for local consumption and export.

Fishing: Fishing is plentiful and fish is still the main source of animal protein. The chief fish caught are shrimp, snapper, carp, eel, and tuna. The surplus is supplied to the international market after domestic demands are met.

Mining: Taiwan produces small amounts of coal, sulfur, copper, gold, marble, dolomite, iron, jade, opal, and coral. Salt is produced by solar evaporation along the southern coast. Petroleum and natural gas exist in small quantities on shore. Energy is principally derived from imported petroleum; three nuclear power plants provide about 40 percent of Taiwan's electricity requirements.

Manufacturing: Taiwan has developed skill-intensive high-technology industries producing pharmaceutical, precision instruments, sophisticated electronics, and information processing systems. Most important manufacturing categories are electronics (calculators, television sets), plastic goods (toys), synthetic yarns, and motor vehicles. Kaohsiung is the chief industrial center with an enormous export-processing zone; it is also one of the world's largest container-handling ports. Taiwan is one of the world's largest manufacturers of grass skiing equipment. Quality, reliability, and the creation of new products is emphasized in Taiwanese manufacturing.

Transportation: There are about 2,900 mi. (4,667 km) of railroad tracks, and about 12,100 mi. (19,473 km) of roads; almost 90 percent of the roads are paved. The Sun Yat-sen Freeway and the electrified trunk railroad extend from Kaohsiung in the southwest to Keelung in the north. Chiang Kai-shek International Airport is in Taoyuan, near Taipei; another international airport at Hsiaokang is near Kaohsiung. There are 12 airports with scheduled flights. Kaohsiung and Keelung are the two largest international seaports. Taipei is served by a rapid transit system, taxis, and buses.

Communication: Some 100 daily newspapers are published in Chinese and English. Taiwan has excellent international and domestic telecommunication services. In the early 1990s there was one radio receiver per 1.5 persons, one television set per three persons, and one telephone per two persons.

Trade: Taiwan ranks among ten leading exporters in the world. The chief imports are electronic and nonelectrical machinery, chemicals, iron and steel, motor vehicles, and crude petroleum. Major import sources are Japan, the United States, Germany, Australia, Hong Kong, and South Korea. The chief export items are data processing equipment, winter garments, radio transmission equipment, plastic goods, footwear, athletic equipment, and synthetic fabrics. Major export destinations are the United States, Hong Kong, Japan, Germany, Singapore, and the Netherlands.

EVERYDAY LIFE

Health: Taiwan has a well-developed hospital system and medical profession. Herbal medicine has been in use in China for thousands of years; roots of flowers like the morning glory and St. John's lily (*wenchu* orchid) are used for their medicinal qualities. Taiwanese pharmacies specialize in both "Western" medicine and traditional Chinese medicine. Acupuncture is an ancient Chinese form of needle therapy. Major diseases are cancer, heart disease, diabetes, liver disease, and hypertensive disease. Life expectancy at 71 years for males and 77 years for females is high. Taiwanese consider exercise basic for good health and longevity. Infant mortality rate at 5.3 per 1,000 is low.

Education: Nine years of compulsory school attendance is required of all children. Preschool is optional; many preschools are private, but tuition is free in most public kindergartens. The elementary grades are one to six and junior high is grades seven through nine. Junior high students must pass a competitive exam to enter high school; high school seniors also must pass an exam before entering college. Special education is provided for handicapped, disabled, or gifted students. The government provides free textbooks in the elementary grades and encourages rural communities to establish schools by giving out grants. There are 11 independent colleges and 16 universities in Taiwan. In the early 1990s the literacy rate was about 93 percent—one of the highest in the world.

Holidays:

> January 1-2, New Year's Day; Founding of the Republic of China Day
> March 29, Youth Day
> April 5, Tomb-Sweeping Day
> May 1, Labor Day
> September 28, Teacher's Day; Birthday of Confucius
> October 10, National Day (Double Tenth Day)
> October 25, Taiwan Retrocession Day
> October 31, Chiang Kai-shek's Birthday
> November 12, Sun Yat-sen's Birthday
> December 25, Constitution Day

Movable holidays (based on the Chinese lunar calendar) are Chinese New Year, Dragon Boat Festival (Poets' Day), and Mid-Autumn Moon Festival.

Food: Seafood is a favorite of Taiwanese. An average meal includes steamed rice, vegetables, and chopped meat or fish. Chinese food is fast becoming a favorite throughout the world for its careful preparation, quick cooking, and imaginative serving. Chopsticks made of bamboo, wood, ivory, plastic, or silver are used to eat food. *Dim sum*, "snacks," are hot, cold, sweet, or salty and include white turnip cakes, fresh shrimp dumplings, and rice pastries. *Yuan hsiao* are small dumplings made of rice with sweet fillings. Street-side vendors sell dried squid, shrimp, seaweed, mushrooms, and other prepared foods such as shark's fin stew, dumplings, and oyster-rice noodles. Chinese green tea is the national drink.

Sports and Recreation: The most popular games are baseball, tennis, biking, soccer, grass skiing, and basketball. Mountain climbing, swimming, fishing, hang gliding, wind surfing, scuba diving, and camping are popular recreations. Tamsui has the oldest golf and country club in Taiwan and one of the most challenging in East Asia. Skiing is popular at Mt. Hohuan in January and February. Martial arts, like *t'ai chi ch'uan*, "shadow boxing," and *shaolin chúan*, are practiced for self-defense and also for their beneficial exercise. (Shaolin chúan is the name of a well-known temple in central China, where the monks developed a special school of boxing.) Traditional games include cock fighting, shuttlecock kicking, jumping rope, and spinning tops. Puppetry is the most popular traditional art. Paper cutting is extremely popular among Taiwanese women.

Social Welfare: The government insurance programs cover about one-third of the people. The labor insurance program covers workers; it provides benefits for injury, disability, birth, death, and old age. Low income families are covered under a separate system of supplementary benefits since 1978. Taiwanese people tend to take care of their elders and unemployed relatives at home.

IMPORTANT DATES

299 B.C.–Poet-statesman Chu Yuan drowns himself in a river to call attention to the lack of government reforms

A.D. 618–The practice of sweeping the tombs of ancestors starts

1206–Genghis Khan establishes the Yuan Dynasty on mainland China

1356–Ming Dynasty is established on mainland China (ends 1644)

1430–Cheng Ho tells the Ming court about his travels in Taiwan

1590–A Portuguese galleon sights the island of Taiwan

1593–Japan tries to occupy Taiwan, but fails

1624–The Dutch settle on Taiwan's southern coast and build three forts

1626–Spanish missionaries arrive; they bring Roman Catholicism from the Philippines

1627–First Protestant missionaries arrive in Taiwan

1638–Manchus take over Taiwan

1642–The Spanish are driven from Taiwan by the Dutch

1658–Koxinga retreats from mainland China and occupies Taiwan

1661–Koxinga ousts the Dutch from the island of Taiwan

1665–The Confucius Temple is built in T'ainan

1684–Manchus get control of Taiwan; T'ainan becomes capital of the island

1721–Taichung city is founded as Tatun by emigrants from mainland China

1831–A Prussian missionary, Karl Gutzlaff, visits Taiwan

1860–The port of Tamsui is opened for foreign trade

1867–An earthquake destroys much of Keelung

1875–A shrine to Koxinga is built at T'ainan

1884–The French bombard Keelung and capture it, for eight months

1886–Taiwan becomes a province of China

1895–The end of the first Sino-Japanese War; China surrenders Taiwan to Japan; Japanese rename Tatun as Taichung and Mt. Yu Shan as *Niitakayama*, "New High Mountain"

1899–Oracle ox bones and tortoise shells with ideographic symbols are excavated in Honan Province on mainland China

1912–The Republic of China (ROC) is established

1945–Japan returns Taiwan to China; Taiwan becomes a province of the Republic of China; the Nationalist government of China becomes a charter member of the United Nations

1947–Anti-Chinese Nationalist violence erupts in Taiwan on February 28, which is brutally suppressed by Nationalist Chinese troops; the present constitution of the ROC is promulgated

1948–Chiang Kai-shek is elected president of ROC by the National Assembly

1949–Kuomintang forces are defeated by the Communist forces; KMT relocates its government from mainland China to Taiwan; Chiang Kai-shek establishes a provisional capital at Taipei; martial law is imposed in Taiwan; Communist People's Republic of China (PRC) is proclaimed on mainland China

1954–A mutual defense treaty is signed between the United States and the Republic of China

1960–The East-West Cross-Island Highway is completed; first feature-length color movies are made; Chiang is elected ROC president for the third time after the constitutional provision on a two-term restriction is removed

1965–The National Palace Museum is opened to the public

1966–Chiang is elected to a fourth term as ROC president and Yen Chia-kan is elected vice-president

1970–The Martyrs Shrine is erected in Taichung

1971–The PRC replaces the ROC on Taiwan as a permanent member of the United Nation's Security Council and Taiwan is no longer a UN member

1972–Legislative elections are held for the first time in 24 years; Chiang Ching-kuo is appointed premier by his father

1973–Taiwan rejects the People's Republic of China's offer to hold discussions on the reunification of China

1975–President Chiang Kai-shek dies; Yen Chia-kan is sworn as president

1978–The National Assembly elects Chiang Ching-kuo as president

1979–The United States switches diplomatic recognition from the ROC to the PRC and terminates the mutual defense treaty; the US has since maintained only "non-governmental" relations with Taiwan

1980–Taiwan is expelled from the International Monetary Fund (IMF) and the World Bank

1981–Taiwan once again rejects a PRC offer for reunification

1983–Elections are held for seats in the Legislative Yuan

1984–The sport of grass skiing is introduced in Taiwan by Germans

1986–A Taiwanese pilot defects to mainland China; dissidents form an opposition party named the Democratic Progressive party (DPP) in defiance of martial law

1987–The government lifts martial law and ends emergency rule; freedom of the press is restored; the 38-year-old ban on visits to mainland China by Taiwanese citizens is repealed; the DPP becomes legal

1988–Mainland Chinese are permitted to visit Taiwan; President Chiang Ching-kuo dies and is succeeded by Lee Teng-hui

1989–The president of Taiwan visits Singapore; pro-democracy demonstrations are violently suppressed in Beijing

1990–The National Affairs Conference (NAC) is convened; President Lee is reelected

1991–Senior members of the three parliamentary bodies are retired (elected before 1947); some 950,000 Taiwanese visit mainland China; all remaining restrictions on freedom of speech, press, and assembly are lifted; elections are held for the 405-member National Assembly; Taiwan becomes a member of the Asia-Pacific Economic Co-Operation forum; Typhoon Ruth hits Taiwan causing considerable damage

1992–The Republic of Korea withdraws recognition from Taiwan and establishes diplomatic relations with the People's Republic of China; the Taiwan government remains recognized by less than 30 countries in the world; Taiwan's first full Legislative Yuan elections are held since 1949, with the DPP taking more than one-third of the popular votes and seats; Taiwan is granted observer status at the General Agreement on Tariffs and Trade

1993–Dr. Lien Chan, a native of Taiwan and a U.S. educated political scientist from the University of Chicago, is appointed premier

1994–Taiwan's government announces that it is ready to lift a two-decade old ban on rice imports if the country is allowed to join GATT

IMPORTANT PEOPLE

Chang Ta-chien (1899-1983), artist; famous for landscape paintings

Cheng Cheng-kung (1624-1662), also known as Koxinga; a Chinese national hero; venerated as a *chun tzu* "perfect man"; fought the Manchus for more than a decade; he is considered the founding father of Chinese civilization on Taiwan

Cheng Chi-lung, a Taiwan-based pirate; assembled the remainder of the Ming forces; father of Koxinga

Cheng Ho (1371-1433), Ming Dynasty magistrate and navigator; led a vast naval expedition (1405-07); in 1430 he reported to the Ming court about Taiwan

Chiang Ching-kuo (1910-88), Chiang Kai-shek's son; president of Taiwan, 1978-88

Chiang Monlin (1886-1964), educator and chairman of the joint commission on rural reconstruction

Chiang Kai-shek (1887-1975), Chinese general and politician; president of Chinese Nationalist government, 1928; president of national government, 1943-49; resumed presidency on Taiwan, 1950-75

Chu Yuan (?-299 B.C.), poet-statesman; drowned himself in a river to call attention to the lack of government reforms; Dragon Boat Festival is held every year in his memory

Confucius (555-479 B.C.), Chinese scholar and sage; his basic ethics are called jen, meaning humanity

Hu Shih (1891-1962), philosopher and president of the Academia Sinica (science)

Lao Tze (6th century B.C.), Chinese philosopher; considered founder of Taoism

Dr. Lee Teng-hui (1923-   ), professor of economics; president of Taiwan since 1988; first native-born president; also governor of Taiwan province for four years, mayor of Taipei, and vice-president of the ROC

Lee Yuan-tseh (1936-   ), winner of the Nobel Prize in chemistry in 1986; president of the Academia Sinica since 1993

Lin Cho-liang (1960-   ), concert violinist; professor at Juilliard School of Music in New York City

Annette Lu Hsiu-lien (1944-   ), feminist and dissident; founder of Taiwan's National Organization of Women (NOW); imprisoned for sedition, 1979-85; chair of 1994 Global Summit of Women as president of Taiwan International Alliance

Peng Ming-min (1924-   ), renowned scholar of international law; professor of political science; author of a proclamation calling for democratic changes and political reforms in 1964; imprisoned for sedition; exiled (in United States) from Taiwan, 1971-92; leads reform movement in Taiwan

Soong Mei-ling (1897-   ), also known as Madame Chiang Kai-shek; wife of Chiang Kai-shek

Dr. Sun Yat-sen (1866-1925), Chinese statesman and revolutionary leader; considered founding father of the Republic of China

Tsiang Ting-fu (1895-1965), historian, ROC ambassador and Chinese delegate to the United Nations and the U.S. in the 1950s and the 1960s

Tung Tso-pin (1895-1963), archaeologist

Wang Yung-Ching, (1917-   ), entrepreneur; builder and board chairman of Formosan Plastic Corporation, Taiwan's largest conglomerate

Wu San-lien (1899-1988), publisher of *Independent Evening Post*, Taiwan's independent and most authoritative newspaper; was influential in forging a new Taiwan

Yen Chia-kan, vice-president, 1966-75; president, 1975-78

Compiled by Chandrika Kaul

INDEX

Page numbers that appear in boldface type indicate illustrations

About the Author

Alice Cromie is an author, journalist, and lecturer known for her travel writing. She is an authority on the American Civil War and is the author of *A Tour Guide of the Civil War*.

Born in Iowa and educated at the universities of Missouri and Texas, Mrs. Cromie now lives in Illinois with her husband, Robert, who is also an author and the former host of *Book Beat*, a television show.

Mrs. Cromie has traveled extensively and is especially fond of the country of Taiwan. This is her first *Enchantment of the World* title.